THE HONE & STRONG
DIARIES OF OLD
MANHATTAN

THE HONE & STRONG
DIARIES OF OLD
MANHATTAN

Edited by

Louis Auchincloss

ABBEVILLE PRESS • PUBLISHERS • NEW YORK

EDITOR: WALTON RAWLS
DESIGNER: JOEL AVIROM
COPY CHIEF: ROBIN JAMES
PRODUCTION SUPERVISOR: HOPE KOTURO

Frontispiece: *Broadway; View from the Foot of City Hall Park* (detail),
watercolor by Axel Leonhard Klinckowstrom, 1819. (MCNY)

In the captions, institutions that have generously permitted the use of their
materials are identified by the following abbreviations:

(MCNY) Museum of the City of New York
(NYHS) New-York Historical Society
(LC) Library of Congress
(SI) Smithsonian Institution
(NYPL) I. N. Phelps Stokes Collection; Miriam & Ira D. Wallach Division
of Art, Prints and Photographs; The New York Public Library; Astor,
Lenox and Tilden Foundations
(MMA) Metropolitan Museum of Art
(WH) White House
(GEH) George Eastman House

First edition.

Library of Congress Cataloging-in-Publication Data

The Hone & Strong diaries of old Manhattan / edited by Louis
    Auchincloss.
    p.   cm.
    Includes index.
    Contents: The Hone diary — The Strong diary.
    ISBN 0-89659-904-3 : $35.00
    1. New York (N.Y.)—Social life and customs. 2. Hone, Philip, 1780–
1851—Diaries.   3. Strong, George Templeton, 1820–1875—Diaries.
4. New York (N.Y.)—History—1775–1865. 5. New York (N.Y.)—History
—1865–1898. I. Auchincloss, Louis. II. Hone, Philip, 1780–1851. Diary
of Philip Hone, 1828–1851. Selections. 1989. III. Strong, George Templeton,
1820–1875. Diary of George Templeton Strong. Selections. 1989.
IV. Title: Hone and Strong diaries of old Manhattan. V. Title: Diaries of old
Manhattan.
F128.44.H79 1989
974.7′103′092—dc20
89-35564
CIP

Contents

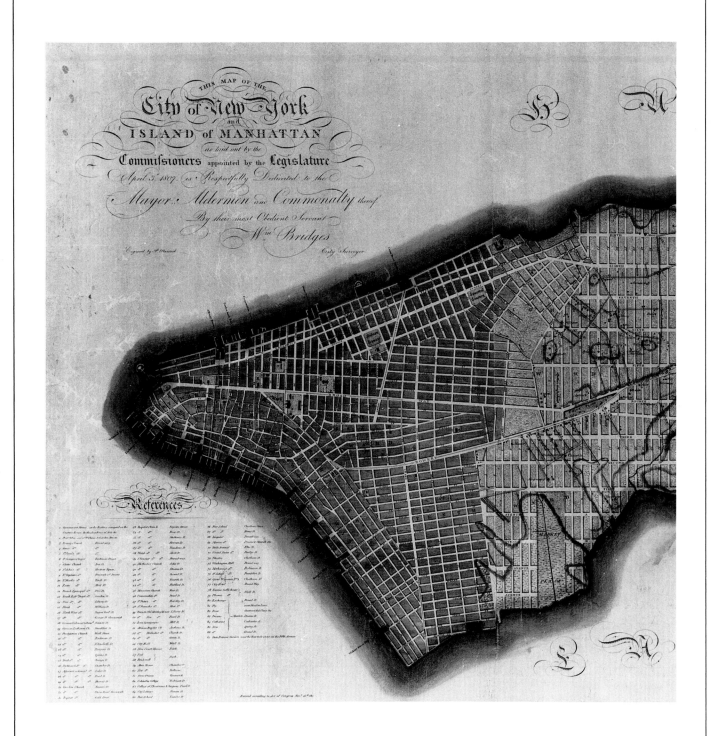

6

Foreword

OPPOSITE: "The Commissioners Map" (detail), engraving by Peter Maverick from an 1807 survey by John Randel, Jr., 1811. The darkened area shows the extent of habitation at the time, perhaps reaching as far uptown as the present Washington Square. The new street and lot grid was laid out from 14th Street all the way to 155th, even though the Common Council judged it might take "years (possibly centuries)" to fill out that vast area. (MCNY)

Nothing is more stressed in the popular histories of New York City than the steady, ineluctable northern crawl of its new buildings from the southern tip of Manhattan, never halting until halted by the Harlem River, by which time the whole of the skinny island (saving the blessed oasis of Central Park) had been densely covered with a thick layer of brownstone. Robert Benchley used to parody nostalgic New Yorkers with the quip: "When I was a boy, the Battery was way uptown." But in 1826, when Philip Hone, having completed his single one-year term as mayor, commenced his famous diary, Bond Street marked the city's northern boundary, the population was still under 200,000, and everyone recognized that William H. Aspinwall, the shipping magnate, had the swellest mansion in town.

If we add on to Hone's diary, which he faithfully kept until his death in 1851, the much-longer one of George Templeton Strong, we are provided with a continuous record of life in the city for a span of fifty years, the period in which New York came of age as a great metropolis. For by Strong's death in 1875 the city had at last broken out of Manhattan into the Bronx (Brooklyn, Queens, and Staten Island were still to join); the population had swelled to well over a million; Wall Street was the undisputed capital of American finance, and the great cultural institutions, the Metropolitan Museum of Art, the American Museum of Natural History, and the Lenox Library had been founded.

It is unfortunate that only half of each of these great diaries has been published. The manuscripts of both are in The New-York Historical Society, waiting for an imaginative publisher or foundation to undertake their editing and printing in full. I cannot claim to have studied these manuscripts sufficiently to be able to state that such an undertaking would be worth the considerable cost, but I can affirm that everywhere I have dipped into them I have found what was omitted every bit as interesting as what has been published. I do not, however, suggest that anyone need reproduce the long extracts from books that Hone transcribed as samples of his favorite reading. Some editing is always necessary.

Hone and Strong were both members of the upper middle class, or what would be called the upper class did we not cling to the old habit of reserving an empty space at the top of our social ladder for an absent aristocracy, and their point of view was definitely that of the substantial property holder. Both men viewed with profound distrust new economic ideas that might tend toward any redistribution of the wealth. And both were inclined to see the increasing swarm of European immigrants, particularly the Irish, as potential if not actual radicals and agitators, and any politicians who catered to them as dangerous demagogues. But political conservatives may still have big hearts, and Hone and Strong shared a profound patriotism and idealism, and strove to improve the society in which they were active and public-spirited citizens. Their enthusiasm for their native city gives color and movement to the vivid diaries they so consciously kept.

View of St. Paul's Church and the Broadway Stages, N.Y., lithograph by Pendleton from a drawing by Hugh Reinagle, 1831. The foot of City Hall Park at about the time Philip Hone started his famous diary. His home is just a few buildings to the north. P. T. Barnum's American Museum is shown at the left, on the corner of Broadway and Ann Street. (MCNY)

Indeed, it seems at times as if these voracious journals were eating up their creators, that the poor diarists had to keep on the run to supply the inexorable pages with their fodder of news. They covered everything that went on in town: the plays and operas and concerts, the charity balls and visits of dignitaries, the circuses and freak shows, the art exhibitions, the fires and riots, the new fads and fashions. They reported the rise and fall of the stock market, the local scandals and crimes, the problems of the struggling schools and cultural institutions and hospitals, the dirty political deals, the moral crusades. Everything was grist for the mills of their personal literature.

What my real aim has been is to make these famous diaries, too bulky in original manuscript and too long even in their printed editions for the casual reader, readily available for the New York City "buff" who likes to read about the past as well as the present of our town. The original diaries are available in photostat at The New-York Historical Society, and Hone's handwriting, like that of so many of his contemporaries in a pre-typewriter age, is as clear as print, but Strong's is almost illegible.

New York builds itself over every generation, and the Landmarks Commission has only recently developed the power to save the few remnants of history we have left. But the avenues, streets, and parks that our diarists refer to are still there, and it is my hope that the contemporary illustrations added to the texts (many of them by Currier & Ives, another great New York institution) will help to recreate the city Hone and Strong criticized but deeply loved.

Louis Auchincloss

Philip
Hone

P hilip Hone (1780–1851) was not born a member of the affluent managerial class of which he became so conspicuous an adornment. He was in fact of humble origin. His father had emigrated from Germany to become a joiner in a small wooden house at the corner of Dutch and John streets. Philip had little formal education, and at sixteen he went to work for his older brother John who in 1797 had launched a successful auction business. In the next two decades Philip worked hard and amassed a small fortune. By 1821, at the age of only forty, he was able to retire and travel in Europe and collect books and pictures. He had reserved the best years of his life for the improvement of his mind and the appreciation of the varied world around him.

But first he had a brief fling at elective politics. He was too much of a conservative Whig to go far in that dawn of the Jacksonian age, but a temporary split in the ranks of the Democratic party's majority resulted in his being elected mayor of the city for a one-year term. When that was over, and reelection seemed out of the question, he confined his political role (with the exception of one unsuccessful bid for the state Senate) to that of counselor on the sidelines. His wide acquaintance among leaders of the day and his sophisticated knowledge of public events resulted in his being frequently consulted by the great Whig leaders, Daniel Webster, Henry Clay, and William H. Seward—the reason for the frequent trips to Washington recorded in his diary.

Free at last of business and active political involvement, he had now the leisure to satisfy his dearest ambition: that of becoming a leader of society. He saw this role in no narrow or purely snobbish sense. He conceived it, on the contrary, as a noble calling, one where he could lead people by high example to the good life, where literature and art, as well as religion and business, would play their proper parts. His exquisite manners and the cultivation that he had acquired from wide reading (he would have gladly surrendered half his wealth, he wrote, for a classical education) made him welcome among the old families of Manhattan, though his single term in office suggests that he may have never developed the common touch.

His diary is important to historians for its picture of New York manners and leaders, but one of its chief delights lies in its reflection of the diarist himself: an early nineteenth-century gentleman of the best sort, with all of his undoubted virtues and all of his equally undoubted prejudices. Hone is sentimental, emotionally patriotic, nostalgic about Revolutionary ideals, gallant but condescending to the ladies, deeply civic, open to progressive ideas and determined to build a greater New York, but still afraid that we have seen better days than we shall see again and that the nation may be going to the dogs because of bad manners, radicals, and the Irish. He is like a character in a Thackeray novel, where the reader rather than the author supplies much of the irony.

He may have been the last man to be able to know personally every one of importance in the United States. Presidents, congressmen, governors, mayors, writers, painters, merchants, educators, scientists, actors, doctors, and lawyers—all are grist for the ever-grinding mill of his insatiable diary.

Hone was happily married to Catharine Dunscomb for fifty years and was the father of three sons, John, Robert, and Philip, and three daughters, Mary, Margaret, and Catharine. All seem to have been close to their father, and all survived him except his favorite, the beautiful but ever ailing Mary, who married wealthy Jones Schermerhorn and died young. John and Robert, both in the drygoods business, needed constant loans of capital from their father, who supplied them generously as long as he could. Descendants of Hone and of his brother John (this editor descends from the latter) are plentiful today, but the direct male line appears to have died out; there are none that I know bearing the surname Hone. Devoted as Hone was to the female members of his family, they were not included in the kind of convivial gourmet dinners that he most enjoyed: the all-male assemblages of the Hone and Kent dinner clubs that foregathered in the dining rooms of their members' homes while the subservient womenfolk (including, no doubt, some of those victims of male chauvinism, the languid Victorian chaise-lounge semi-invalids) retired upstairs away from the toasts and laughter. The Hone Club dinners were limited to soup, fish, oysters, four meat dishes, with a dessert of fruit, ice-cream, and jelly, to accord

Residence of Philip Hone, Esq., and American Hotel, Broadway, 1831. Hone's home, 235 Broadway, is shown in this print taken from the first picture book of New York: Theodore S. Fay's *Views in the City of New-York and Its Environs*, published by Peabody & Co., 1831-32, whose shop is at 233, next to the Hone residence. (MCNY)

with the gravity of the pre-announced topics of discussion: the American Revolution and its heroes; the framers of the constitution; New York and her improvements; the mercantile advancement of the city; the Union and its powers.

Hone on the subject of President Andrew Jackson sounds like a Republican speaking of Franklin D. Roosevelt, exactly a century later: "That such a man should have governed this great country with a rule more absolute than that of any hereditary monarch of Europe and that the people should not only have submitted to it, but upheld and supported him in his encroachments upon their rights, and his disregard of the Constitution and the laws, will equally occasion the surprise and indignation of future generations."

In 1850, the year before he died, Hone was as socially active as ever, but there may have been some slight impairment of memory. The entry for October 30 reads:

> The great affair came off last evening, at the elegant mansion of Samuel S. Howland, whose daughter Catharine was united to Mr. Charles H. Russell in the "holy bonds of Matrimony." . . . The affair was brilliant; the company embracing besides all the relations and connections of the two families, a great concourse of distinguished ladies and gentlemen, strangers and citizens who witnessed the ceremony and partook of an excellent supper.

No mention is made of the fact that the bride was the diarist's great-niece, granddaughter of his brother John, or that the groom, a widower of fifty-four and the father-in-law of the diarist's son Robert, was twenty-five years older than his young wife. Hone even gets the bride's name wrong; it was not Catharine but Caroline. Or was it not a failure of memory, but a reflection of the feeling of the time that a young lady would do very well with a rich and distinguished husband, even if almost twice her age? And indeed the Russell marriage was a happy one and produced six children.

Hone died in 1851, his last days clouded by gloomy forebodings as to the future of his beloved nation. He was one of those who was equally opposed to secessionists and abolitionists. His entry for December 31, 1850 reads:

> The last day of this eventful year,—a year in which the bad passions of men have been employed to counteract the beneficent designs of Providence; when the prosperity of the country and the happiness of the people have been in danger of sinking beneath the violence of sectional jealousy and the rude attacks of factious demagogues who would rend asunder the bonds of union which have hitherto raised us to an unprecedented state of prosperity and set at naught the Constitution and laws on which our fathers laid the foundations of the Republic.

The Hone Diary

1830

Hone traveled frequently to Boston, Philadelphia, Baltimore, and Washington. His trip to Baltimore this year took him three days and involved a constant changing from stage to steamboat. The route was New Brunswick, Trenton, Philadelphia, Baltimore.

MARCH 15, MONDAY   BALTIMORE

The Washington Monument in Howard Park is nearly finished, being surmounted by the figure of the Father of his Country. It is well proportioned, and the material, a fine gray granite, is beautiful. The situation, on the slope of a hill, is well chosen to display the grandeur and simplicity of this noble specimen of art. I paid this morning a visit which I have long been wishing for to the venerable Charles Carroll, the only surviving signer of the Declaration of Independence. He will be 94 years of age next September. His faculties are very little impaired, except his sight, which within the last few months has failed a little and deprived him of the pleasure of reading at all times, which he has heretofore enjoyed. He is gay, cheerful, polite, and talkative. He described to me his manner of living. He takes a cold bath every morning in the summer, plunging headlong into it; rides on horseback from eight to twelve miles; drinks water at dinner; has never drunk spirituous liquors at any period of his life, but drinks a glass or two of Madeira wine every day, and sometimes champagne and claret; takes as much exercises as possible; goes to bed at nine o'clock, and rises before day.

OPPOSITE: *View of Baltimore*, lithograph by Nathaniel Currier, 1848.

Charles Carroll of Carrollton (detail), a painting by William James Hubard, 1830. This portrait of the last surviving signer of the Declaration of Independence was painted the same year that Hone visited him. (MMA)

1831

Hone occupied a handsome mansion at 235 Broadway, just below the corner of Park Place. Directly south was the American Hotel, and, farther down, St. Paul's Chapel. To the northeast, across Broadway, was City Hall, at the head of a triangular park. It was from the window of his dressing room that Hone witnessed, on April 20, the fisticuffs between William Cullen Bryant, the poet and journalist, and one of his critics.

Daniel Webster, the great orator, constitutional lawyer, and Whig senator from Massachusetts, was a lifelong friend of Hone and probably the man he most admired in American political life. The Hone Club, a gentlemen's dinner group that met in the residences of its members (the wives and daughters being dismissed upstairs), commissioned his portrait, which was moved from house to house for stipulated periods.

MARCH 22, TUESDAY   NEW YORK CITY

A splendid dinner was given this day by a number of our citizens to the Hon. Daniel Webster for his able defense of the Constitution. The company consisted of about 250 of the most respectable persons in the city. Chancellor Kent presided, with Messrs Jay, Greenway, and John Hone as vice-presidents. . . . The sixth and eighth toasts (Daniel Webster; John Marshall) were introduced by the president with appropriate remarks in his best manner. They were excellent and in singular good taste. After the applause which followed the sixth had subsided, Mr. Webster arose and made an address of an hour and a half, which no one who heard it will ever forget. It was patriotic, fervent, eloquent, imbued with no party violence, purely American; it was "our country, our whole country, and nothing but our country." There were many fine things in it. I remarked most particularly the following beautiful train of metaphor. The orator in portraying the character of Hamilton eulogized his exertions to raise the credit of the country in its day of peril, and the system of finance which he established, and said:

> He struck the flinty rock, and copious streams of revenue flowed from it. He touched the lifeless corpse of public credit, and it sprang upon its feet a living body. The fabled birth of Minerva was not more sudden than that which his head produced.

OPPOSITE: A preliminary drawing by Alexander Jackson Davis for a lithograph of the American Hotel, with Hone's home in the center. (MCNY)

APRIL 20, WEDNESDAY

While I was shaving this morning at eight o'clock I witnessed from the front windows an encounter in the street nearly opposite between William C. Bryant, one of the editors of the *Evening Post,* and William L. Stone, editor of the *Commercial Advertiser.* The former commenced the attack by striking Stone over the head with a cowskin; after a few blows the parties closed and the whip was wrested from Bryant and carried off by Stone. When I saw them first, two younger persons were engaged, but soon discontinued their fight. A crowd soon closed in and separated the combatants.

This disgraceful affair originated in several publications which appeared in the two papers respecting a volunteer toast which was given at Mr. Burgess's dinner, reflecting upon the editors of the *Evening Post* and of the *Courier and Enquirer.* The former paper charged Stone with being the author of the toast, which he denied and demanded a disclaimer, which was either refused or given with a bad grace, and he charged the editors in his paper of Saturday with falsehood. Bryant waited for Stone this morning, and took satisfaction in the manner above related.

1832

This was the year of the cholera, a worldwide epidemic that killed 20,000 persons in France alone. It hit New York in the summer, and 100,000 persons fled the city.

Martin Van Buren, until 1831 secretary of state, had been named minister to England and had sailed to his post only to learn that the Senate, under the influence of anti-Jacksonians, had refused to confirm his appointment, and he returned to New York from Liverpool.

Fanny Kemble, the English actress, made a hit at the Park Theatre, which had opened in 1798, across from City Hall Park. She later married a South Carolina planter, Pierce Butler.

FEBRUARY 18, SATURDAY

The president of the Senate and the Speaker of the House of Representatives have addressed a note, by direction of the joint committee for celebrating the centennial anniversary of the birth of Washington, to John A. Washington, proprietor of Mount Vernon, requesting permission to remove his remains to the Capitol on the day of the celebration. This request he has refused, properly, I think. Let Congress purchase the estate and erect a mausoleum on the spot where the remains of the Father of his Country now rest, but do not place them in the Capitol, where they may hereafter be exposed to the contamination of the neighborhood of some demagogue who may be raised to that distinction by party prejudice and not by patriotism.

The Tomb and Shade of Washington, lithograph by Currier & Ives, n.d. (MCNY)

MARCH 25, SUNDAY   BALTIMORE

Mr. and Mrs. Caton having called this morning to invite us, we passed an hour or two delightfully at their house this evening. The family were all present. Mr. [Charles] Carroll was cheerful and talkative and enjoyed himself very much until nine o'clock, when according to his uniform practice he took the arm of Mr. McTavish and left the room. I feel while in the presence of this venerable man as if I were permitted to converse with one of the patriarchs revisiting the land which in days long gone he had enriched with his patriotic counsels. He is in his ninety-sixth year; his hearing is defective and his memory of recent events imperfect. But he presents a beautiful example of the close of a well-spent life, serene, cheerful, and happy; prepared, it would seem, to "take his rest, with all his country's honors blest." It is very probable I shall never again see him after the present visit, and this reflection enhanced the value of the delightful hour I have just passed in his company. I made Mary take a seat by his side, and she has it to say that she conversed some time with the last surviving signer of the immortal Declaration of Independence. Would to God we had such a race of men in high places at this eventful period of our country's affairs. But Providence took care of us in their days, and as the Scottish ballad says, "It aye will again."

JULY 3, TUESDAY   NEW YORK CITY

The devil is in the doctors again. Whenever cases occur in which the public safety requires union, confidence, and good temper, the members of that factious profession are sure to fall out among themselves and the public health is sacrificed to the support of theoretical opinions. The medical society has been at issue with the Board of Health, who presume to doubt if the cholera, such as prevailed in Asia and prevails now in Quebec, really exists in this city. The doctors have published their reports without the sanction of the board, a most unjustifiable measure which would be attended with fatal consequences if the people relied more upon them.

JULY 4, WEDNESDAY

It is a lovely day, but very different from all the previous anniversaries of independence. The alarm about the cholera has prevented all the usual jollification under the public authority. There are no booths in Broadway, the parade which was ordered here has been countermanded, no corporation dinner, and no ringing of bells. Some troops are marching about the street, "upon their own hook," I suppose. Most of the stores are closed, and there is a pretty smart cannonade of crackers by the boys, but it is not a regular Fourth of July. The Board of Health reports to-day twenty new cases and eleven deaths since noon yesterday. The disease is here in all its violence and will increase. God grant that its ravages may be confined, and its visit short! I wrote to-day for the girls to return from Hyde Park forthwith. They are all going to Rockaway. Catharine is greatly alarmed, and we are to ascertain whether the seashore is a place of safety.

JULY 5, FRIDAY

Mr. Martin Van Buren arrived last evening in the packet ship *New York* from Liverpool, sailed June 1. His party in this city had made arrangements to receive him on his arrival, and committees waited upon him for the purpose. Processions were to have been formed and speeches made, but with proper delicacy he declined the honor, alleging as a reason the alarm existing in the city on account of the cholera.

JULY 16, MONDAY   ROCKAWAY

The accounts of the cholera in New York have become dreadfully alarming, and it is spreading rapidly over the whole country. Albany, the towns on the river, different parts of New Jersey and Connecticut, are becoming successively the theater of its ravages. The following reports of the Board of Health for the last three days show a progressive increase: Saturday the 14th, 115 new cases, 66 deaths; Sunday, 133 new cases, 74 deaths; Monday, 163 new cases, 94 deaths.

I left Rockaway after breakfast this morning and came to the city. Miss Lewis accompanied me. The alarm is very great but the streets are more lively than I expected. I went to Wall Street and transacted some business; there was a considerable number of persons on 'Change, and I saw but few stores closed on my walk. Great alarm has been occasioned by the sudden death of George E. Smith, alderman of the Fourth Ward. He attended the board on Saturday night until eleven o'clock, was taken ill with cholera at three in the morning, and died in seven hours. But I have learned that although he was an active man and a vigilant magistrate, he was habitually addicted to the intemperate use of ardent liquor. I hear many dreadful stories of cholera cases. The last of last week a man was found in the road at Harlem, who had died of cholera. A coroner's inquest was called, and of twenty persons, jury and witnesses, who were present, nine are now dead. John Aspinwall told me this story.

A cholera broadside dated July 18, 1832, that lists the addresses of those stricken with the disease and notes whether they have died or recovered. (MCNY)

July 31, Tuesday

I came into town this morning with Mr. Abraham Ogden. The eastern section of the city is nearly deserted, and business of every description appears to be at a stand. Broadway and the lower part of the city is yet tolerably lively, and Wall Street and other parts "where the merchants do congregate" retains much of its usual bustle and animation.

August 8, Wednesday

Cholera report: 82 new cases, 21 deaths. This dreadful disease has reached Philadelphia, where it rages with violence nearly equal to that which has desolated New York. I found a letter this morning from Mr. Joseph Watson, in which he gives me some particulars. The greatest mortality has been in the Arch Street Prison and in the Hospital.

August 27, Monday

My wife, my daughter Margaret, and I came up from Rockaway this morning, and brought Joanna Anthon with us. I presume I have taken my leave of Rockaway for the season. The change in the appearance of the city is very great. The favorable reports of cholera, and the pleasant weather, have brought thousands of the refugees back to their homes. Business has revived, the streets are lively and animated, and everything seems to be resuming its wonted appearance. We are very cautious, however. Beef and mutton are allowed, but vegetables and fruit are strictly interdicted. The peaches and melons in vain throw their fragrance around; we look at them, we sigh for their enjoyment—but we don't touch them. I am well of my diarrhoea, and I find it exceedingly difficult to resist the temptation. It is too much for the frailty of human nature and I am off to the Springs to-morrow to get out of the way.

The English actress Fanny
Kemble, with whom Hone dined
on September 15, 1832, shown in
her role as Belvidera, 1830.
(MCNY)

The Park Theater, a watercolor by Alexander Jackson Davis. The theater, which opened in 1798, was directly across City Hall Park from Hone's residence. It had burned in 1820, but it was re-opened in 1821, only to burn again in 1848 and not be rebuilt. (MCNY)

SEPTEMBER 15, SATURDAY

Miss [Fanny] Kemble, like all young persons who have become celebrated, has many and strong admirers. But many dislike her on first acquaintance. Her manners are somewhat singular. Allowance should be made for the peculiarity of her situation, just arrived among strangers, with a consciousness that she is viewed as one of the lions of the day, and as such the object more of curiosity than of affection. Her behavior would be attributed naturally to timidity, were it not that at times she appears to be perfectly self-possessed. She talks well, but will only talk when, and to whom she chooses. She sat at my side at dinner, and I certainly had no reason to complain of her, for I lost my dinner in listening to her and in endeavoring to make myself agreeable. She has certainly an air of indifference and nonchalance not at all calculated to make her a favorite with the beaux. Indeed, Henry Hone and I think that she prefers married men.

Her fault appears to be an ungracious manner of receiving the advances of those who desire to pay her attention. This may proceed from the novelty of her situation, and may be soon removed. But now is her time to make friends if she wants them. She sang and played for us in the evening. Her voice is not sweet, but has great force and pathos. I am confirmed in my opinion that she has astonishing requisites for the stage. Her features separately are not good, but combined they make a face of great and powerful expression. She is said to resemble her aunt, Mrs. Siddons. I am of opinion that she does not like her profession. It is not her favorite theme of conversation; necessity, rather than choice, has led her to adopt it. Her father is a gentleman of fine manners and dignified deportment, somewhat stiff—for he is a Kemble—but evidently well bred and accustomed to good society.

1833

Hone, a loyal Whig, or National Republican, regarded the election of the Democrat Andrew Jackson as a national calamity and the triumph of mob rule, but he nonetheless attended Jackson's second inaugural and described in detail the re-elected president's popular visit to New York in June. Jackson's administration was marked by reform movements—the president demanded free public schools, more rights for women, better working conditions in factories, and the abolition of slavery. But revisionist historians hardly find him such a radical as to justify the excessive apprehensions of Hone and his propertied friends. Hone, like many Whigs, was inclined to find a radical under every bed, as conservatives of our day are inclined to find communists. To Hone, any extension of the suffrage meant an extension of the power of the poor, and hence a threat to the rich; the poor were symbolized in his mind by the growing mass of Irish immigrants whom he saw as rude, tough, drunken peasants with a peculiar aptitude for controlling municipal politics.

OPPOSITE: *Andrew Jackson, Seventh President of the United States*, lithograph by Currier & Ives, n.d. (MCNY)

The inauguration of Andrew Jackson as President and Martin Van Buren as Vice-President of the United States took place at noon in the hall of the House of Representatives. I went up at eleven o'clock and formed one of an immense crowd who thronged the approach to every door. The wind was very high and the severity of the cold unmitigated, so that the time spent in waiting was not particularly agreeable. The President and Vice-President and their cortège arrived at 12 o'clock, and soon afterwards the door was opened, when I was carried in with the ruffianly crowd, but never got farther than the little vestibule in front of the chamber. I am told that the President delivered an inaugural address, and that the oath was administered by the venerable Chief Justice. The address is published in handbills: it is well done, not too long, and well adapted to the state of public affairs.

The President held a levee after the ceremony of inauguration, and crowds went to the palace, I among the rest. But shortly before I arrived he had been compelled to retire from exhaustion, and the people were returning. He looks exceedingly feeble. If it were delicate and respectful to bet on such a subject, I would bet large odds that he does not outlive the present term of his office.

I have engaged my place in the stage for Wednesday next, but it is amusing to see the strife to get seats; every vehicle is engaged for several days ahead. I hope to get to Baltimore on Wednesday, but "when go thence?"—for the severity of the weather has caused a suspension of the traveling by steamboat, and I won't go by land, that's flat.

MARCH 6, WEDNESDAY   BALTIMORE

I left Washington after breakfast, and contrary to my fears, had a pleasant ride. The weather continued very cold; the ground is covered with snow, but hard frozen, and not so deep as to make the wheeling difficult. Baltimore is full of homeward bound travelers, detained by the obstruction of the navigation, many of whom cannot find where to lay their heads. I am better off. I have a good chamber, with a parlor adjoining, which is jointly occupied by Washington Irving and myself. I had not been in the house at Barnum's fifteen minutes before I received invitations for four dinners, which will carry me to the end of my visit, unless I should continue weatherbound beyond that time.

MARCH 11, MONDAY

Irving will remain a few days, and then pass a week in Philadelphia. I have found him a most delightful companion. He is cheerful, gay, talkative, and appears to be no longer subject to those moody fits which formerly obscured his fine intellect at times, as the dark clouds flit across the face of the brightest summer's day. Irving finds himself quite at his ease in Baltimore. He is caressed by the women and honored by the men, "the observed of all observers," and I think he "carries his faculties meekly about him." He gives himself no airs, is lively without conceit, and instructive without pedantry. I consider it fortunate that I invited him to be my roommate, and I presume he does also.

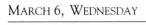

ABOVE: Portrait engraving of the author Washington Irving, America's first professional man of letters. Hone shared a parlor with him in Baltimore. (MCNY)

BELOW: *The Washington Irving Dinner*, lithograph by Swett, 1832. Hone attended the dinner and noted in his diary for May 30, 1832, that it was "a regular Knickerbocker affair; there were old New Yorkers and their descendants in goodly numbers who are seldom seen at such places, and among the invited guests were many distinguished men." (MCNY)

APRIL 1, MONDAY   NEW YORK CITY

Audubon [John James] the celebrated ornithologist, called upon me a day or two since with letters of introduction from Mr. Quincy, president of Harvard College, and Col. Perkins of Boston. He is about setting out on one of his enterprising excursions to the coast of Labrador, in pursuit of information to illustrate his favorite science, to which he is devoted with the ardor of a lover to his mistress. He is an interesting man of about 55 years of age, modest in his deportment, possessing general intelligence, an acute mind, and great enthusiasm. His work on the birds of North America, in which he is now engaged, is probably the most splendid book ever published. I have seen several of the numbers in the Library of Congress; it will require nine years to complete it, and will cost $800; all the drawings are executed by himself or under his special superintendence.

JUNE 12, WEDNESDAY

This has been a day of jubilee in New York. The note of preparation has been sounding in our ears for a week past. The Man of the People (for he is such in a greater degree than any who has gone before him) slept last night at Trenton and was to make his triumphal entry to-day; and with the exception of Lafayette's arrival, we have never witnessed such a scene.

I had the honor to receive from the Corporation an invitation to attend them as an escort on board the *North America* steamboat. The company assembled at nine o'clock and started immediately; the superb vessel was fitted up in admirable style, draped in flags of all nations. The weather was beautiful. All the shipping in the harbor displayed their colors. The *Ohio, Hercules,* and *Rufus King,* all filled with passengers, accompanied the *North America,* and our Capt. Crittenden took the lead as commodore of the fleet. Our company consisted of between three hundred and four hundred, who were quite generally persons of high standing and respectability.

We arrived at Perth Amboy a few minutes after 11 o'clock. The vessels were anchored off a short distance from shore, where we lay until one o'clock, at which time the steamboat *York* arrived from Brunswick with the President, and was received with cheers. After landing him a few ceremonies were performed, and he came on board our vessel and was received in due form by the

OPPOSITE: *John James Audubon,* painting by John Syme, 1826. When Audubon called on Hone, he had not long returned from Edinburgh, where he had finally arranged for the publication of his *Birds of America.* (WH)

U. S. SHIP OF THE LINE OHIO, *104 Guns.*

committee of arrangements as the guest of New York. The President was accompanied by Mr. McLane, the Secretary of State, Gov. Cass, etc. When the introductions were concluded, the flotilla was set in motion and the whole party was seated at the most splendid dinner which was ever seen on board a vessel. The whole of the cabin from stem to stern formed a beautiful saloon, decorated with flowers and otherwise ornamented with beautiful taste. The dinner was excellent, and the wines served up in as fine order as if a party of twenty persons only were to be provided for. Among other delicacies there were fourteen fresh salmon well cooked and in prime order. Niblo provided the dinner, and the little man certainly covered himself with glory. On entering the Narrows the noble Forts Hamilton and Diamond saluted in fine style, and the reports of their heavy guns broke up the dinner party and brought the company upon deck.

OPPOSITE: *U.S. Ship of the Line Ohio,* lithograph by Nathaniel Currier, 1847. The *Ohio,* one of nine ships-of-the-line authorized by Congress in 1816 (following the War of 1812), was an escort vessel for President Jackson's visit. Hone mentions that the flotilla received a salute from Governors Island, whose old fort is shown to the left of the ship. (MCNY)

RIGHT: *Niblo's Garden, Rear View,* engraving, 1820. The dinner for President Jackson, which Hone praised so highly, was catered from this well-known establishment. (MCNY)

We were saluted from the quarantine ground, from the revenue cutter, and other vessels lying there, and from Governor's Island. The bay on our approach was covered with vessels of every size and description. The landing took place on the wharf at Castle Garden, where the President was received by the mayor, and conducted to the great saloon, handsomely prepared for the occasion. Thus far everything was well conducted, but it was impossible to preserve order. The wharves and housetops and vessels were covered with people; the troops were drawn up on the Battery. The President mounted a horse provided for him and reviewed them, but from the moment of landing all was confusion.

The President now took up the line of march to the City Hall, and I made the best of my way home. Broadway from the Battery to the Park formed a solid mass of men, women, and children, who greeted their favorite with cheers, shouts, and waving of scarfs and handkerchiefs. He was received at the Hall by Gov. Marcy and his staff, and after receiving the marching salute of the troops from the platform fronting the Park, was conveyed in a barouche, accompanied by the Vice-President, Governor, and Mayor, to his lodgings at the American Hotel next to my house, where a guard of honor was stationed to receive him. He reached his lodgings at seven o'clock. Boardman, the keeper of the hotel, has fitted up his apartments in superb style.

American Hotel, No. 229 Broadway, New York, Opposite the Park, a lithograph by Alexander Jackson Davis that shows where President Jackson lodged on his visit to New York. (MCNY)

June 13, Thursday

The President is certainly the most popular man we have ever known. Washington was not so much so. His acts were popular, because all descriptions of men were ready to acknowledge him the "Father of His Country." But he was superior to the homage of the populace, too dignified, too grave for their liking, and men could not approach him with familiarity. Here is a man who suits them exactly. He has a kind expression for each—the same to all, no doubt, but each thinks it intended for himself. His manners are certainly good, and he makes the most of them. He is a *gourmand* of adulation, and by the assistance of the populace has persuaded himself that no man ever lived in the country to whom the country was so much indebted. Talk of him as the second Washington! It won't do now; Washington was only the first Jackson.

Poor [John Quincy] Adams used to visit New York during his presidency. The papers, to be sure, announced his arrival; but he was welcomed by no shouts, no crowd thronged around his portals, no huzzas rent the air when he made his appearance, and yet posterity, more just than ourselves, will acknowledge him to have been in all the qualifications which constitute his fitness to fill the office of a ruler of this great republic, twenty times superior to Jackson. He wanted tact. He gave the toast of *Ebony and Topaz,* the ungracious offspring of a mind loaded with study and unskillful in adaptation. And the other, in a moment when we were all anxious to save the country. . . . and when we doubted what his course would be, gave in a happy moment his toast, "The Union—it must be preserved." It made a difference of five hundred thousand votes. Adams is the wisest man, the best scholar, the most accomplished statesman; but Jackson has most tact. So huzza for Jackson!

OVERLEAF: *Staten Island and The Narrows,* lithograph by Currier & Ives, 1861. As the presidential flotilla passed through The Narrows, Hone noted that Fort Hamilton, at right, and Fort Diamond, in the center, "saluted in fine style." (MCNY)

1834

The mayorality election was the first popular election in the history of the city. The Whigs put up a weak candidate, Gulian Verplanck; Tammany nominated Cornelius Lawrence, a member of Congress. The latter was an easy winner, but only after some riotous demonstrations against the vested interests by what Hone indignantly described as Irishmen "of the lowest class." Similar disorders attended the national elections in November, making it a year of violence and class hatred known as the "Year of Riots."

OPPOSITE: **The interior of an Irish (and Democratic) saloon at No. 488 Pearl Street that was used as a voting place on election days.** *(Harper's)*

RIGHT: **Hone mentions several times how effective the "Irishmen" were in controlling New York's elections.** *Harper's Weekly* **illustrates "How they vote in the 7th Ward." (MCNY)**

JANUARY 23, THURSDAY

This was the most brilliant affair we have seen in a long time. "Mr. Ray at home, Thursday, 23d inst. Quadrilles at nine o'clock." The very cards gave promise of *quelque chose distinguée.* The fashionable world rushed with excited expectation to the gay scene, and none were disappointed. Mr. Ray has the finest house in New York, and it is furnished and fitted up in a style of the utmost magnificence—painted ceilings, gilded moldings, rich satin ottomans, curtains in the last Parisian taste, and splendid mirrors, which reflect and multiply all the *rays,* great and small. On this occasion, all the science of all the accomplished *artistes* was put in requisition; decorators, cooks, and confectioners vied with each other, and each in his vocation seemed to have produced the *ne plus ultra;* and unlike other entertainments of the kind, the spirit of jealousy and emulation cannot be excited to an inconvenient degree, for . . . no person possesses such a house and very few the means to show it off in the same style. . . .

The diary records that "respectable persons were beaten and
trampled in the mud," and
Harper's shows "rioters robbing
citizens." (MCNY)

APRIL 9, WEDNESDAY

There were several riots yesterday in the Sixth Ward, which have been repeated this morning. Respectable persons were beaten and trampled in the mud. Joseph Strong, the former alderman of the ward, is charged with having instigated and encouraged the rioters. The mayor and sheriff were called upon and interfered promptly and vigorously, and order was restored. Similar disturbances took place at the same polls this morning, and many persons were seriously hurt.

APRIL 10, THURSDAY

Last day of the election; dreadful riots between the Irish and the Americans have again disturbed the public peace. I happened to be a witness of the disgraceful scene which commenced the warfare. On leaving the hospital at noon, Mr. Goodhue and I, observing the miniature frigate which our people have drawn through the streets during the election standing before the Masonic Hall, we went over and ascended to the large room, where several persons of the Whig Party were assembled, all perfectly quiet, as were the crowd in the streets, when suddenly the alarm was given, and a band of Irishmen of the lowest class came out of Duane Street from the Sixth Ward poll, armed with clubs, and commenced a savage attack upon all about the ship and the hall. There was much severe fighting and many persons were wounded and knocked down. The Irishmen then retired and the frigate was drawn away, but in a few minutes the mob returned with a strong reënforcement, and the fight was renewed with the most unrelenting barbarity. The mayor arrived with a strong body of watchmen, but they were attacked and overcome, and many of the watchmen are severely wounded. Eight of them were carried to the hospital, where I went to visit them.

The mayor has ordered out Col. Sanford's regiment and a troop of horse, and proper measures have been taken to preserve order, but we apprehend a dreadful night. This outrage has been instigated by a few men in the Sixth Ward—George D. Strong, Abraham LeRoy, Dr. Rhinelander, Preserved Fish, and a few like him. Let them answer it.

July 10, Thursday

There has been of late great excitement in consequence of the proceedings of a set of fanatics who are determined to emancipate all the slaves by a *coup de main,* and have held meetings in which black men and women have been introduced. These meetings have been attended with tumult and violence, especially one which was held on Friday evening at the Chatham Street Chapel. Arthur Tappan and his brother Lewis have been conspicuous in these proceedings, and the mob last night, after exhausting their rage at the Bowery Theater, went down in a body to the house of the latter gentlemen in Rose Street, broke into the house, destroyed the windows and made a bonfire of the furniture in the street. The police at length interfered, rather tardily, I should think; but the diabolical spirit which prompted this outrage is not quenched, and I apprehend we shall see more of it.

The conduct of the Abolitionists has been very indiscreet, but their number has been too small to give reasonable ground of alarm; and this attack upon one of their leaders will add to their strength by enabling them to raise the cry of persecution.

JULY 12, SATURDAY

The riots continued last night. Some troops were out, but the mob had made so many points of attack that they completed in many instances their work of destruction before the police and military could be brought to the spot, and they appear to have been emboldened by an opinion which was industriously spread among them that the troops could not fire without orders from the Governor as commander in chief. This is erroneous, as they may find to their cost. The church of Dr. Cox, corner of Laight and Varick Streets, was nearly demolished, as was that of the Rev. Mr. Ludlow in Spring Street, and the residences of those gentlemen were attacked and rifled and the furniture burnt in the street. The Episcopal African church in Center Street and the house of the respectable pastor, Peter Williams, were also destroyed, and many of the houses of black people, particularly in Leonard Street and the Five Points, shared the same fate.

JULY 14, MONDAY

The efficient measures of the police, aided by a force of two or three thousand uniformed militia with a strong body of citizens organized as special constables, succeeded in preserving the peace of the city. Crowds of people assembled at different places on Saturday night, but no violence was attempted, and there is reason to hope the riots are at an end.

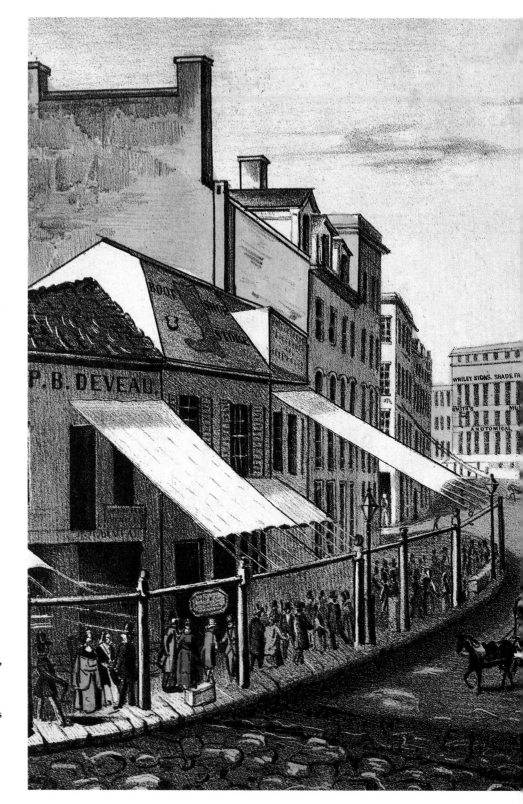

Chatham Square, New York,
lithograph by Nathaniel Currier,
c. 1847. This view is northeast
from Chatham Street, which is
now Park Row, and shows the
troops out in force, which seems
to have been a common occurrence in Hone's day. (MCNY)

JULY 18, FRIDAY

Edmund Charles Genet [Citizen Genêt] died on Wednesday last at his residence at Schodack, Rensselaer County. He was at one time an important personage. He came as Minister of the French Republic to this country, and acted as became the representative of the madmen who, under the name of liberty, were destroying their country and crushing the people. Nothing but the firmness of Washington prevented Genet from enlisting the people of this country in the cause of the French mob. . . . I remember well when a boy seeing Genet, then Minister, dancing the carmagnole with a red cap on his head in the street before Mr. Bradley's boarding-house in Maiden Lane, surrounded by the sans-culotte crews of the French frigates which lay in our harbor, and cheered by thousands of our citizens not less extravagant than they.

NOVEMBER 6, THURSDAY

The triumph was celebrated last night by the worshipers of Jackson with the refinement and forbearance which might have been expected. I had been taken in the morning with an attack of vertigo and headache, which confined me to the house nearly the whole day, but I made out to walk up in the evening to Masonic Hall, where the news I received was not calculated to make me feel better. I returned home much indisposed, and retired to bed at an early hour, where I was kept awake during the greater part of the night by the unmanly insults of the ruffian crew from Tammany Hall, who came over to my door every half hour and saluted me with groans and hisses. This continued till past three o'clock, and for what? Because I have exercised the right . . . of expressing my disapprobation of a course of measures which I conceive to be dangerous to the liberties of the people, and inimical to the free institutions of my native land. This I have done with truth, zeal, and firmness, but always, I trust, with decorum and propriety; and for this I have been insulted and annoyed. I have for many years sacrificed my comfort, exhausted my time, and abridged my enjoyments by a devotion to the service of my fellow citizens. A member of all the public institutions, charitable, public-spirited, or patriotic, where time was to be lost, labor performed, and no pay to be had; my own affairs neglected, and my money frequently poured out like water; the friend and patron of the workingmen, without regard to party. And now my reward is found in the revilings of a mob of midnight ruffians, among whom, I have no doubt, were some of the very men whom I have assisted to support, to the exclusion of others who are proud to acknowledge themselves my personal and political friends. I believe I am rightly served.

Tammany Hall on Election Night,
engraving by J. McNevin.
(Harper's)

1835

December witnessed the greatest fire in the history of the city, a conflagration that could be seen as far as New Haven and that destroyed the greater portion of lower Manhattan.

November 4, Wednesday

I witnessed yesterday at Matteawan a sight which I have frequently read and heard of, but never saw until now—a flight of wild pigeons. They came from the west, and crossing the valley where I was, passed the top of the mountains and went to the south and east. The air was filled with them; their undulation was like the long waves of the ocean in a calm, and the fluttering of their wings made a noise like the crackling of fire among dry leaves or thorns. Sometimes the mighty army was scarcely visible in the bright blue sky, and in an instant a descent of astonishing rapidity brought them so low that if we had been provided with guns, it would have been literally "every shot a pigeon." During the whole morning small detachments of the main body were seen flying about in the passes of the mountains. Every man and boy of the Matteawaneans who could get a gun, and was willing to lose part of his day's work in the factory, sallied out on murder bent; a *feu de joie* was kept up during the day; and the pigeon pie became an unexpected dish on many a table. I am glad I have seen this show. I shall be able hereafter to talk "pigeon" with Audubon, in his own language.

DECEMBER 17, THURSDAY

How shall I record the events of last night, or how attempt to describe the most awful calamity which has ever visited these United States? The greatest loss by fire that has ever been known, with the exception perhaps of the conflagration of Moscow, and that was an incidental concomitant of war. I am fatigued in body, disturbed in mind, and my fancy filled with images of horror which my pen is inadequate to describe. Nearly one half of the first ward is in ashes; 500 to 700 stores, which with their contents are valued at $20,000,000 to $40,000,000, are now lying in an indistinguishable mass of ruins. There is not perhaps in the world the same space of ground covered by so great an amount of real and personal property as the scene of this dreadful conflagration. The fire broke out at nine o'clock last evening. I was waiting in the library when the alarm was given and went immediately down. The night was intensely cold, which was one cause of the unprecedented progress of the flames, for the water froze in the hydrants, and the engines and their hose could not be worked without great difficulty. The firemen, too, had been on duty all last night, and were almost incapable of performing their usual services.

The fire originated in the store of Comstock & Adams in Merchant Street, a narrow crooked street, filled with high stores lately erected and occupied by dry goods and hardware merchants, which led from Hanover to Pearl Street. When I arrived at the spot the scene exceeded all description; the progress of the flames, like flashes of lightning, communicated in every direction, and a few minutes sufficed to level the lofty edifices on every side. It had crossed the block to Pearl Street. I perceived that the store of my son John (Brown & Hone) was in danger, and made the best of my way by Front Street around the Old Slip to the spot. We succeeded in getting out the stock of valuable dry goods, but they were put in the square, and in the course of the night our labors were rendered unavailing, for the fire reached and destroyed them, with a great part of all which were saved from the neighboring stores; this part of Pearl Street consisted of dry goods stores, with stocks of immense value of which little or nothing was saved. At this period the flames were unmanageable, and the crowd, including the firemen, appeared to look on with the apathy of despair, and the destruction continued until it reached Coenties Slip, in that direction, and Wall Street down to the river, including all South Street and Water Street; while to the west, Exchange Street, including all Post's stores, Lord's beautiful row, William Street, Beaver and Stone Streets, were destroyed. The splendid edifice erected a few years since by the liberality of the merchants,

OVERLEAF: *The Great Conflagration . . . from Coenties' Slip,* lithograph by Nathaniel Currier, 1835. A firsthand view of the city's greatest fire, which wiped out the remnants of New York's Dutch past, destroying some 600 buildings below Wall Street. (MCNY)

known as the Merchants' Exchange, and one of the ornaments of the city, took fire in the rear, and is now a heap of ruins. The façade and magnificent marble columns fronting on Wall Street are all that remains of this noble building, and resemble the ruins of an ancient temple rather than the new and beautiful resort of the merchants. When the dome of this edifice fell in, the sight was awfully grand. In its fall it demolished the statue of Hamilton executed by Ball Hughes, which was erected in the rotunda only eight months ago by the public spirit of the merchants.

I have been alarmed by some of the signs of the times which this calamity has brought forth: the miserable wretches who prowled about the ruins, and became beastly drunk on the champagne and other wines and liquors with which the streets and wharves were lined, seemed to exult in the misfortune, and such expressions were heard as "Ah! They'll make no more five per cent dividends!" and "This will make the aristocracy haul in their horns!" Poor deluded wretches, little do they know that their own horns "live and move and have their being" in these very horns of the aristocracy, as their instigators teach them to call it. This cant is the very text from which their leaders teach their deluded followers. It forms part of the warfare of the poor against the rich; a warfare which is destined, I fear, to break the hearts of some of the politicians of Tammany Hall, who have used these men to answer a temporary purpose, and find now that the dogs they have taught to bark will bite them as soon as their political opponents.

These remarks are not so much the result of what I have heard of the conduct and conversation of the rabble at the fire as of what I witnessed this afternoon at the Bank for Savings. There was an evident run upon the bank by a gang of low Irishmen, who demanded their money in a peremptory and threatening manner. At this season there is usually a great preponderance of deposits over the drafts, the first of January being the day on which the balances are made up for the semi-annual dividend. All the sums now drawn lose nearly six months interest, which the bank gains. These Irishmen, however, insisted upon having their money, and when they received it were evidently disappointed and would fain have put it back again. This class of men are the most ignorant, and consequently the most obstinate white men in the world, and I have seen enough to satisfy me that, with few exceptions, ignorance and vice go together. These men, rejoicing in the calamity which has ruined so many institutions and individuals, thought it a fine opportunity to use the power which their dirty money gave them, to add to the general distress, and sought to embarrass this excellent institution, which has been established for the sole benefit of the poor. . . . These Irishmen, strangers among us, without a feeling of pa-

Alexander Hamilton **by Ball Hughes, the original plaster model of the 15-foot marble statue destroyed in the burning of the Merchants' Exchange, now in the Museum of the City of New York. (MCNY)**

Ruins of the Merchants' Exchange, lithograph by Nathaniel Currier, 1835. (MCNY)

The Life of a Fireman. The Fire,
lithograph by Currier & Ives,
1854. Firefighting was a social
and fraternal diversion at this
time, as the various companies
raced against each other to be
first in putting water on a fire.
Not only did they pull their
pumpers by hand to the site, but
in connecting their hoses to the
city's fireplugs they often had
to fight "plug-uglies" sent ahead
by rival companies, and then
pump up enough pressure to send
the water onto the fire.
(MCNY)

triotism or affection in common with American citizens, decide the elections in the city of New York. They make Presidents and Governors, and they send men to represent us in the councils of the nation, and what is worse than all, their importance in these matters is derived from the use which is made of them by political demagogues, who despise the tools they work with. Let them look to it; the time may not be very distant when the same brogue which they have instructed to shout "Hurrah for Jackson!" shall be used to impart additional horror to the cry of "Down with the natives!"

OPPOSITE: *The Life of a Fireman. The Race—"Jump her boys, jump her!,"* lithograph by Currier & Ives, 1854. A fire company races past City Hall, dragging both its hand pumper and hose carriage. Because of the constant danger of fire, a watchtower was erected just behind City Hall, but that did not save the cupola of the adjacent edifice, which was destroyed by fire in 1858. (MCNY)

RIGHT: Getting out the vote. A Democratic ward heeler sees to it that "Tim Maloney" exercises his franchise early. *(Harper's Weekly)*

1836

Charles H. Russell, later president of the Bank of Commerce, had built a house on Great Jones Street near where Hone was shortly to build and move. Russell's daughter Eliza married Hone's son Robert.

DECEMBER 30, FRIDAY

I went this evening to a party at Mrs. Charles H. Russell's, given in honor of the bride, Mrs. William H. Russell. The splendid apartments of this fine house are well adapted to an evening party, and everything was very handsome on this occasion. The home is lighted with gas, and the quantity consumed being greater than common, it gave out suddenly in the midst of a cotillion. "Darkness overspread the land." This accident occasioned great merriment to the company, and some embarrasment to the host and hostess, but a fresh supply of gas was obtained, and in a short time the fair dancers were again "tripping it on the light fantastic toe."

Gas is a handsome light, in a large room like Mr. Russell's, on an occasion of this kind, but liable (I should think) at all times to give the company the slip, and illy calculated for the ordinary uses of a family.

1837

Hone was delighted to see the end of Andrew Jackson's administration. The new president, Martin Van Buren, was also a Democrat, and a loyal Jacksonian to boot, but he was a New Yorker (the first president from the state) and a "gentleman," and Hone had hopes for him.

The year marked the beginnings of Hone's financial troubles, which were to plague him for the rest of his life, although he always managed to maintain a comfortable, even a luxurious style of living. He had had, however, to borrow considerable sums for the construction of his new house on Great Jones Street at Broadway, and the Panic of 1837 found him lamenting the increasing tightness of money: "the usurers are fattening upon their two and one half and three per cent a month, which they make indirectly by the medium of bills and exchange. The poor borrowers are forced to pay for the ingenuity of the lenders in avoiding the penalties of the usury laws. . . ."

JANUARY 3, TUESDAY

Mr. Lawrence, the Mayor, kept open house yesterday, according to custom from time immemorable, but the manners as well as the times have sadly changed. Formerly gentlemen visited the mayor, saluted him by an honest shake of the hand, paid him the compliment of the day, and took their leave; one out of twenty perhaps taking a single glass of wine or cherry bounce and a morsel of pound cake or New Year's cookies. But that respectable functionary is now considered the mayor of a party, and the rabble considering him "hail fellow well met," use his house as a Five Points tavern. Mr. Lawrence has been much annoyed on former occasions, but the scene yesterday defies description. At ten o'clock the doors were beset by a crowd of importunate *sovereigns*, some of whom had already laid the foundations of *regal* glory and expected to become *royally* drunk at the hospitable house of His Honor. The rush was tremendous; the tables were taken by storm, the bottles emptied in a moment. Confusion, noise, and quarreling ensued, until the mayor with the assistance of his police cleared the house and locked the doors, which were not reopened until every eatable and drinkable were removed, and a little decency and order restored.

I called soon after this change had taken place. The mayor related the circumstances to me with strong indignation, and I hope the evil will be remedied hereafter. All this comes of Mr. Lawrence being the mayor of a party and not of the city. Every scamp who has bawled out "Huzza for Lawrence" and "Down With the Whigs" considered himself authorized to use him and his house and furniture at his pleasure; to wear his hat in his presence, to smoke and spit upon his carpet, to devour his beef and turkey, and wipe his greasy fingers upon the curtains, to get drunk with his liquor, and discharge the reckoning with riotous shouts of "Huzza for our mayor." *We* put him in and *we* are entitled to the use of him. Mr. Lawrence (party man as he is) is too much of a gentleman to submit to this, and sometimes wishes his constituents and his office all to the devil, if I am not greatly mistaken, and if he rejects (as he has now done) their kind tokens of brotherly affection, they will be for sending him there ere long, and will look out for somebody of their own class less troubled than him with aristocratical notions of decency, order, and sobriety.

JANUARY 31, TUESDAY

A fine large steamboat was launched yesterday. She belongs to Capt. Cobb, and is intended for an English packet. This experiment is looked for with some solicitude on both sides of the water; it was frequently the subject of conversation when I was in England last summer. It would be presumptuous to express a doubt as to the success of any new experiments in the mechanical arts in our days of successful enterprise, but I do presume to doubt, for I cannot conceive of an improvement in safety or convenience over such noble craft as the *England* or the *Sylvie de Grasse.* In light head-winds and moderate weather a steamer would go wheezing and puffing alongside of the proudest ship in the British or American navy, and passing, laugh her to scorn; but let the ocean be lashed into such a foam as I saw it several times in coming home, and let the waves run high as the topmast, and how is this long stiff vessel, over-burthened with the weight of machinery, with a burning volcano in her bowels, to ride on the crested billows and sink again into their dark, deep caverns? It may answer— and if it does, heigh for the Downs, the Mersey, or the Seine in ten days.

MARCH 4, SATURDAY

This is the end of Gen. Jackson's administration—the most disastrous in the annals of the country, and one which will excite "the special wonder" of posterity. That such a man should have governed this great country, with a rule more absolute than that of any hereditary monarch of Europe, and that the people should not only have submitted to it, but upheld and supported him in his encroachments upon their rights, and his disregard of the Constitution and the laws, will equally occasion the surprise and indignation of future generations. Or their indifference will prove that the love of liberty and independence is no longer an attribute of our people, and that the patriotic labors of the men of the Revolution have sunk like water in the sands, and that the vaunted rights of the people are considered by them as a "cunningly devised fable."

This is also the commencement of Mr. Van Buren's reign, the first New York President. He has said that it was "honor enough to have served under such a chief," and will no doubt for a time speak with reverence of the ladder by which he has risen to the summit of ambitious hopes; but I do not despair of him. He will be a party President, but he is too much of a gentleman to be governed by the rabble who surrounded his predecessor and administered to his bad passions. As a man, a gentleman, and a friend I have great respect for Mr. Van Buren.

This is a dark and melancholy day in the annals of my family. Brown & Hone stopped payment to-day, and called a meeting of their creditors. My eldest son has lost the capital I gave him, and I am implicated as endorser for them to a fearful amount. The pressure of the times, the immense amount they have paid of extra interest, and the almost total failure of remittances have been the causes of their ruin. This is a heavy blow for me, and added to the difficulty I experience in raising money on my property to meet my own engagements, almost breaks me down, but I have the consolation to know, and the public cannot fail to know it also, that the good name which it has been the object of my life to establish, cannot be compromised in this matter.

May 11, Thursday

A dead calm has succeeded the stormy weather of Wall Street and the other places of active business. All is still as death. No business is transacted, no bargains made, no negotiations entered into; men's spirits are better because the danger of universal ruin is thought to be less imminent. A slight ray of hope is to be seen in countenances where despair only dwelt for the last fortnight, but all is wrapped up in uncertainty. Nobody can foretell the course matters will take. The fever is broken, but the patient lies in a sort of syncope, exhausted by the violence of the disease and the severity of the remedies.

The Times, lithograph by Edward
W. Clay, 1837. One artist's commentary on the hardships brought
about by the Panic of 1837. The
head in the clouds is said to represent ex-President Jackson.
(MCNY)

MAY 27, SATURDAY

I dined with the governing committee of the Union Club; the first dinner in the clubhouse, No. 343 Broadway. The house will be open to the subscribers on Thursday next. It is well fitted up, the furniture neat and handsome, good servants, and above all a most *recherché chef de cuisine.* Subscribers will get a better dinner and at one half the cost than at any hotel in town. It is a great resource for bachelors, and "men about town," but I do not see how we married men can be induced to leave our comfortable homes and families to dine *en garçon* at the club, even under the temptation of M. Julien's *bon diner à la Paris.*

OCTOBER 26, THURSDAY

Black Hawk, hand-colored wood engraving. Black Hawk was the former chief of the confederated tribes of Sauks and Foxes, and Hone found him "silent, surly, and picturesque." (MCNY)

Broadway in the neighborhood of the City Hotel has been crowded for the two last days by curious spectators, watching to obtain an occasional glimpse of a large party of Indians who, after having made a treaty at Washington by which their "broad lands" are diminished in quantity the trifling amount of a million and a quarter of acres, are now making a tour of the principal cities, receiving presents and being stared at for the benefit of theaters, fairs, and lectures. There are two tribes, amounting in all to seventy individuals. The Sauks and Foxes, who constitute the most important part of the deputation, are at the City Hotel, and the Sioux at the National, opposite; for these two tribes are not on a friendly footing, and their white keepers do not think it expedient to get up a real war fight for the edification of the spectators.

I went to see the Sauks and Foxes this morning, and finding Mr. Daniel Jackson there, who is a sort of agent for the tribes, was introduced to the principal chiefs. The whole party, warriors, squaws, and papooses, were seated or lying on the ground; most of them employed in opening and dividing sundry pieces of colored cord, such as is used for hanging pictures, which had been presented to them at the fair of the American Institute and with which they appeared much pleased. Keokuk, the chief of the confederated tribes of Sauks and Foxes, and his favorite squaw, were seated on a small carpet separate from the rest. He is a fine-looking elderly man, of intelligent countenance and dignified deportment. I have heard Gen. [Winfield] Scott speak of him; he thinks him a great man. In the expedition against the tribes, a few years since, Keokuk was friendly to the whites and opposed to Black Hawk, who was then the principal chief. Black Hawk is with the party at present, but appears to have

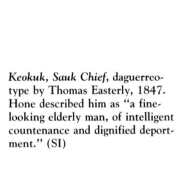

Keokuk, Sauk Chief, daguerreotype by Thomas Easterly, 1847.
Hone described him as "a fine-
looking elderly man, of intelligent
countenance and dignified deportment." (SI)

lost caste. He sits with his son in one corner of the square, enveloped in a
bright scarlet blanket, silent, surly, and picturesque. The son is a majestic man,
aged about thirty, one of the noblest figures I ever saw—a perfect Ajax Telamon.
I shook hands with these Herculeses and Apollos of the woods. They are generally very stout and athletic, with immense lower limbs, but their arms and
hands are delicate and small. Keokuk's hand feels like the hand of a woman,
while that of young Black Hawk is not so large as mine; and yet in other
respects I am much inferior in size and strength to either of them. This characteristic may be accounted for from the circumstance that they perform no
manual labor, and the stoutness and great size of their feet is owing to their
constant exercise in the chase and other field exercises. I was interested greatly
in this visit. The Indians went to Boston at four o'clock this afternoon.

1838

Several duels are described in the course of the diary, but the bloodiest was the outcome of an attack in the House of Representatives on James Watson Webb, editor of the New York *Courier and Inquirer,* by Congressman Jonathan Cilley of Maine. Webb enlisted W. J. Graves, of Kentucky, to deliver his challenge to Cilley, but the latter refused the challenge on the grounds that Webb was not a gentleman. Since Webb, a fiery individual who had been engaged in other affairs of honor, was the son of an aide-de-camp to General Washington, one presumes that Cilley's fastidiousness was prompted more by his opponent's profession than his birth. Graves insisted on fighting him in Webb's place, and so the unfortunate Cilley paid for his snobbishness with his life; Graves killed him on the third shot. Webb's son Seward later married the heiress Eliza Vanderbilt.

JANUARY 26, FRIDAY

My wife, daughter Margaret, Jones and I dined with Mr. and Mrs. Olmstead. The dinner was quite *à la française*. The table, covered with confectionery and gew-gaws, looked like one of the shops down Broadway in the Christmas holidays, but not an eatable thing. The dishes were all handed round; in my opinion a most unsatisfactory mode of proceeding in relation to this important part of the business of a man's life. One does not know how to choose, because you are ignorant of what is coming next, or whether anything more is coming. Your conversation is interrupted every minute by greasy dishes thrust between your head and that of your next neighbor, and it is more expensive than the old mode of shewing a handsome dinner to your guests and leaving them free to choose. It will not do. This French influence must be resisted. Give us the nice French dishes, *fricandeau de veau, perdrix au choux,* and *côtelettes à la province,* but let us see what we are to have.

A dreadful affair had happened at Washington to-day, which only came to my knowledge a few minutes before I left Washington this morning. Mr. Webb, the editor of the *Courier and Enquirer,* was attacked with great violence in the House of Representatives by Mr. Cilley of Maine. . . . Webb was of our party to Washington, and soon after his arrival took measures, it appears, to obtain satisfaction. He applied to Mr. Curtis and Mr. Draper to bear his challenge, both of whom very properly refused. He then called upon Mr. Graves of Kentucky, a very fine fellow, who has been with us almost constantly, and he unfortunately consented. He called upon Mr. Cilley, who refused to accept the challenge, on the ground that Webb was not a gentleman, and moreover, that he was not bound to account for words spoken in debate; upon which Mr. Graves, according to the ridiculous code of honor which governs these gentlemen, insisted upon his fighting him, and after some negotiation it was agreed that they should fight this day. The first suspicion I had of what was going on arose from my meeting Webb in the passage at Gadsby's, about eleven o'clock, when I told him I was going to take leave of Mr. Clay, who lives in the same house with Mr. Graves; on which he said that Mr. Clay, not knowing of the extra train of cars at noon, had gone to Baltimore early in the morning. I went, however, to their lodgings, inquired for Mr. Graves, and was told by a servant that he had gone to Baltimore; but on inquiry found that Mr. Clay was at home, and went to his room, where I saw and took leave of him. This circumstance, together with the mysterious appearance of things at our lodgings, caused me to make inquiry, and I found that Graves and Cilley had gone out to fight with rifles at eighty yards' distance, the former with Mr. Wise and the latter with Gen. Jones, of Wisconsin, as seconds; both adepts in this damnable practice, who would carry things to the utmost extremity, and who are said to have gone armed for the purpose of shooting any person who might come upon the ground to prevent this most unnatural combat.

The friends of Graves, who is a gallant and amiable gentleman, who has his wife here and his children at home, are doing everything to prevent the meeting and bring about a reconciliation; and Webb is much distressed at being the cause of his engaging in this quarrel, which he had nothing to do with; and much reason I think he has. This unhappy affair has caused a gloom among our friends, and prevented the members of Congress from coming on to the public dinner prepared for us in Baltimore.

FEBRUARY 25, SUNDAY

I heard early this morning of the fatal termination of this savage *rencontre*. Mr. Cilley was killed on the third fire. It was reported that Webb and Mr. Duncan, of Ohio, were to fight to-day; but this was contradicted by a letter which I received this evening from Charles King, of which the following is an extract: "The fatal issue of the duel of yesterday has caused a deep sensation. There will not be, however, in my opinion, any more fighting. Webb is truly and deeply distressed. He will remain here till Tuesday, rather so as not to appear to avoid any consequences, than because there are consequences to be apprehended. Graves is, of course, sobered and saddened, though with the consciousness that he had done all that he could have done to avoid fighting. They fought about five o'clock, on the Annapolis road, and fired three times; the third shot from Graves passed into the cavity of Mr. Cilley's stomach. He placed his hand on the wound, made a convulsive movement to his second, fell, and died without uttering a word. It is singular that Cilley, who in practicing the day before had shot eleven balls in succession into a space not bigger than your hand, did not hit Graves at all. So confident were Mr. Cilley's political friends that Graves would be killed, that in the House during the day there was, it is said, manifest exultation at the idea. Some washerwoman or servant told Mrs. Crittenden, in the hearing of Mrs. Graves, that Mr. Graves had gone out to fight, and she had to pass five mortal hours in all the agony of suspense. Mr. Clay, whom I saw in his bed this morning, told me he had had an interview with her, so fearful that it had absolutely kept him awake all night, and made him so sick and nervous this morning, from the mere recollection of it, that he cannot get up. The event of Mr. Cilley's death will be announced to-morrow. The funeral will then take place, and of course both houses will adjourn. It is not impossible that after the death is announced some discussion may arise upon the manner of the death, and some attempt be made to censure the practice generally, and perhaps in this particular case even."

The *Great Western* (for such is the rather awkward name of this noble steamer) came up from Sandy Hook about two o'clock, passed around the *Sirius*, then lying at anchor off the Battery, and proceeding up the East River, hauled into Pike Slip. She is much larger than her avant-courier, being the largest vessel propelled by steam which has yet made her appearance in the waters of Europe. Her registered measurement is 1,604 tons, length 234 feet, breadth from out to out of the paddle-boxes 58 feet, with her engines and machinery of 450 horse-power. She is commanded by Lieut. Hoskin, of the royal navy, and owned by the Great Western Steamship Navigation Company. She sailed from Bristol on the 8th instant, four days later than the departure of the *Sirius* from Cork, performing thus her voyage, under the disadvantages of new machinery and a prevalence of head-winds, in fifteen days.

The city was in a ferment during the day from the arrival of these two interesting strangers. The Battery and adjacent streets were crowded with curious spectators, and the water covered with boats, conveying obtrusive visitors on board. The committee of arrangements of the Corporation have fixed upon to-morrow, at one o'clock for the two Houses, with their guests, to visit the *Sirius*, where a collation will be prepared for them, on which occasion her commander, Lieut. Roberts, is to receive the freedom of the city.

The passengers on board the two vessels speak in the highest terms of the convenience, steadiness, and apparent safety of the new mode of conveyance across the ocean. Everybody is so enamored of it that for a while it will supersede the New York packets—the noblest vessels that ever floated in the merchant service. Our countrymen, "studious of change and pleased with novelty," will rush forward to visit the shores of Europe instead of resorting to Virginia or Saratoga Springs; and steamers will continue to be the fashion until some more dashing adventurer of the go-ahead tribe shall demonstrate the practicability of balloon navigation, and gratify their impatience on a voyage *over,* and not *upon,* the blue waters in two days instead of as many weeks, thereby escaping the rocks and shoals and headlands which continue yet to fright the minds of timid passengers and cautious navigators. Then they may soar above the dangers of icebergs, and look down with contempt upon the Goodwin Sands or Hempstead beach. As for me, I am still skeptical on the subject.

Arrival of the Great Western Steam Ship, Off New York on Monday 23rd April 1838. The *Sirius*, also mentioned by Hone, was the first British steamer to attempt crossing the Atlantic, followed four days later by the *Great Western*. (NYPL)

OVERLEAF: *New York, View from Brooklyn Heights*, lithograph by Nathaniel Currier, 1849. The busy East River side of Manhattan, where the *Great Western* tied up off Pike Slip. (MCNY)

APRIL 27, FRIDAY

The vessel exceeds my expectations. Her steam engine of 400 horse-power, and the other machinery are upon a magnificent scale, and the accommodations for passengers in the best possible taste: the principal saloon is surrounded by forty-two staterooms, sufficiently capacious. The ornaments are of the quaint, old-fashioned style, and the panels are decorated by exquisite paintings, in the costumes of the reign of Louis XV, which give to the whole of this beautiful apartment the appearance of a cabinet of old Dresden china. One of the greatest advantages which this saloon has over the cabins of the packets consists in the height of the ceiling, which affords light and air equal to a well-proportioned dining room or parlor on shore.

JULY 3, TUESDAY

Two of these beautiful animals [giraffes] are being exhibited in a lot on Broadway below Prince Street; the place is handsomely fitted up, and great numbers of persons pay their respects to the distinguished strangers. The giraffes or ca-

The Majestic and Graceful Giraffes, or Cameleopards, 1838. "A drawing made in the beautiful pavillion, No. 509 Broadway, where hundreds daily resort to gaze with delight upon these elegant quadrupeds, the first ever seen in America." Hone was among the visitors on July 3, 1838. (MMA)

meleopards, as they are called (I like the first name best), were taken by one of our Yankee brethren in the interior of Southern Africa. They are the only survivors of eleven who were taken, and have been brought to this country at a very great expense.

AUGUST 9, THURSDAY

I saw in one of the papers the death announced at New Haven of Henry Bedlow, aged 71 years, an old beau who at one time made a great noise in New York. This man, then about 24 years old, was tried for a rape on a Miss Sawyer, stepdaughter of Callahan, a pilot, who lived in Gold Street near my father's. He was acquitted, as I dare say he ought to have been; but her father being well known amongst the seafaring people, and the case, if not a rape, being an aggravated one of seduction, the popular indignation was excited to the highest pitch. A mob collected and pulled down the house to which the libertine had decoyed his victim, a famous brothel kept by a Mother Carey in Beekman Street at the corner of Theater Alley, on the very spot where I built the Clinton Hotel. Well do I remember, although the occurrence took place nearly fifty years ago, sitting in the branches of one of the large buttonwood trees in the burial ground of the Brick Presbyterian Church, opposite the scene of action, and enjoying the dispersion of "Mother Carey's chickens," the destruction of mahogany tables and looking glasses. These excesses did not stop here, for the mob, once excited, continued their riotous proceedings several successive nights, and many houses of ill-fame in other parts of the city were demolished and their miserable inmates driven naked and houseless into the streets.

DECEMBER 8, SATURDAY

We had to dine with us to-day Mr. Christopher Hughes, American *chargé* at Stockholm, Col. Webb, Mr. William B. Astor, and Dr. Francis. Whilst we were at dinner there was a ring at the street doorbell. The boy Daniel went out and found nobody there; but there was a basket on the sill of the door, which he brought into the dining room, and it was found to contain a lovely infant, apparently about a week old, stowed away nicely in soft cotton. It had on a clean worked muslin frock, lace cap, its underclothes new and perfectly clean, a locket on the neck which opened with a spring and contained a lock of dark hair; the whole covered nicely with a piece of new flannel, and a label pinned on the breast on which was written, in a female hand, Alfred G. Douglas. It was one of the sweetest babies I ever saw; apparently healthy. It did not cry during the time we had it, but lay in a placid, dozing state, and occasionally, on the approach of the light, opened its little, sparkling eyes, and seemed satisfied with the company into which it had been so strangely introduced. Poor little innocent—abandoned by its natural protector, and thrown at its entrance into life upon the sympathy of a selfish world, to be exposed, if it should live, to the sneers and taunts of uncharitable illegitimacy! How often in his future life may the bitter wish swell in his heart and rise to his lips, that those eyes which now opened so mildly upon me whilst I was gazing upon his innocent face had been forever closed. My feelings were strongly interested, and I felt inclined at first to take in and cherish the little stranger; but this was strongly opposed by the company, who urged, very properly, that in that case I would have twenty more such outlets to my benevolence. I reflected, moreover, that if the little urchin should turn out bad, he would prove a troublesome inmate; and if intelligent and good, by the time he became an object of my affection the rightful owners might come and take him away. So John Stotes was summoned, and sent off with the little wanderer to the almshouse.

The group in the kitchen which surrounded the basket, before John took it away, would have furnished a capital subject for a painter. There was the elegant diplomat, the inquisitive doctor, the bluff editor, and the calculating millionaire; my wife and daughters, standing like the daughters of Pharaoh over the infant Moses in the bulrushes—all interested, but differently affected, the maids shoving forward to get a last peep; little Emily, the black cook, ever and anon showing her white teeth; James and Dannie in the background, wondering that so great a fuss should be made about so small a matter; and John, wrapped up in his characteristically neat overcoat, waiting, with all the dignified composure which marks his demeanor, to receive his interesting charge and convey it to its destination.

This affair ended, we returned to the dinner table, the game and oysters cold, but our hearts warm; other topics soon engrossed us, and it was near midnight when we broke up.

1839

President Van Buren, still in Hone's good graces, visited the city and received Hone when the ex-mayor called on him at his hotel. The president, as a Democrat and a supporter of the populist Andrew Jackson, was anathema to the conservative Whigs. Hone now felt that Van Buren had forfeited his right to the respect of "men of all parties" by his announcement that his visit to New York was intended for his own political friends. "As he baked, so he must brew."

This year saw the demolition of Trinity Church, the second of that name to occupy the site on Broadway at the foot of Wall Street. It was soon to be replaced by the present structure designed by Richard Upjohn. Hone comments on the discovery of the remains of Lady Cornbury in the demolition of the foundations of the church. She had been buried there in 1706, as wife of the royal governor. Her husband, a first cousin of Queen Anne, was a notorious homosexual and transvestite, who, according to a dubious legend, used to wear women's robes in presiding over the City Council to represent more appropriately his royal female relative.

Hone has little sympathy with the refusal of the tenants of the vast Manor of Rensselaer to pay their rents to the young Stephen Van Rensselaer, son-in-law of Hone's friend the shipping magnate Samuel Shaw Howland, but the brutal repression of this near rebellion shocked the legislature in Albany and led to the amelioration of the almost feudal conditions in which the tenants had lived and worked.

FEBRUARY 4, MONDAY

My son John left home a fortnight ago to attend to some business at Spencer, Tioga County, and returned this evening. His journey has been most disastrous, and the poor fellow has suffered severely from cold, hunger, fatigue, and every other discomfort that attends traveling in winter. After transacting his business at Spencer and Owego, he started in the mail for Utica, was overtaken by a snowstorm, nearly frozen to death, and unable to proceed, carried nearly lifeless to a log hut, where he was brought to by kind but rough treatment; he was fed upon salt fish and potatoes, not twice laid, as the sailors call it, but several times. He got on as far as Cortland village in Cortland County, from whence he wrote us a letter which might pass for an additional chapter to the lamentations of Jeremiah.

MAY 6, MONDAY

I went on Saturday evening to a meeting of the Kent Club at David B. Ogden's. These have been pleasant reunions throughout the winter. The club consists of judges and lawyers, who meet and sup at each other's houses on Saturday evenings in succession; distinguished strangers are invited, and a few laymen, in which last number it has been my good fortune to be frequently included. I have not always been able to attend when invited, but when I have the conversation of these learned "luminaries of law" has greatly instructed and delighted me. The evening is usually divided equally between wisdom and joviality. Until ten o'clock they talk law and science and philosophy, and then the scene changes to the supper-table, where Blackstone gives place to Heidsick, reports of champagne bottles are preferred to law reports, and the merits of oyster pâtés and charlotte russe are alone summed up.

AUGUST 5, MONDAY

In the number of arrivals during my absence is the President of the United States and Mr. Secretary Forsyth, with Mr. Edward P. Livingston and a few others of the faithful.

The President came here Thursday last. He was met some distance from the village by a cavalcade, and followed to his quarters in the United States Hotel (our house) by a motley group. The Whigs say it was a slim concern, and the Locos say otherwise. But here he is, conducting himself with his usual politeness, and making the best of everything, as he is wont to do. I called upon him yesterday immediately after my arrival, and was most graciously received. He hoped I would pass an occasional spare half-hour in his apartment. He has been civil to my wife, and sends his bottle to her and me to drink with him at dinner. I have studied to treat him with all the respect due to his high station and the regard I feel for an old friend, and I acknowledge the kindness with which my advances have been received. This conduct has been pursued by most of the gentlemen, political opponents as well as political adherents; but there has been one exception, on the part of a lady, which in my judgment was equally at variance with good taste and proper feeling. The evening of the President's arrival, whilst he was engaged in playing the gallant to the ladies in the great saloon, he espied Mrs. De Witt Clinton, and crossing the floor, extended his hand to her. This lady, who gives herself a great many airs, has been boasting of her intention to insult him, and on his friendly approach, in the view of the whole company, she folded her arms, gave him a scornful look, and turned off. Mr. Van Buren has too much tact to be disconcerted by such a piece of rudeness, and Mrs. Clinton's conduct has not been justified by any person whom I have heard speak of it.

AUGUST 28, MONDAY

I went yesterday morning to St. Thomas's church, where I heard from Dr. Hawks a glorious sermon; in the afternoon to St. Bartholomew's.

We are vagrants now on Sundays, poor old Trinity being nearly razed to the ground, and a new church to be erected on the same spot, which will require two or three years to complete. We shall be compelled during that time to hire a pew in one of the uptown churches or quarter upon our friends.

When the committee of the vestry of Trinity Church began with the edifice, it was intended to repair and remodel the interior only, leaving the venerable exterior and the noble dark-looking spire in their original integrity. But in the progress of the work the building was found to be in such a state of decay as to be rendered irreparable, and the time-honored temple of the Lord, the parish church of New York, the nucleus of Episcopacy, was doomed to destruction. I found on my return to the city a shapeless heap of ruins on the spot where my imperfect devotions have been performed for the last thirty-seven years. It occasions melancholy reflections to see the dark mass of ruins still overlooking the magnificent temples of Mammon in Wall Street, and to think of the changes which have occurred there during the time the venerable spire which is now removed has thrown its shadow over the place "where merchants most do congregate."

May I not also see in this dilapidation a type of my own decay and speedily approaching removal? When I first went to Trinity Church I was young, ardent, and full of hopes, capable and industrious, and I should now be ungrateful not to acknowledge that in most cases my hopes were realized and my industry rewarded; but the storms within the last three years have beaten upon me, the timbers are decayed, the spire no longer "like a tall bully lifts its head," and the vestry has no funds to rebuild me.

Night-Fall, St. Thomas's Church,
watercolor by George Harvey, c.
1837. Hone attended this church
at Broadway and Houston Street
during the time that Trinity
Church was being demolished
and rebuilt. (MCNY)

DECEMBER 4, WEDNESDAY

I went this morning by invitation of M. François Gouraud to see a collection of the views made by the wonderful process lately discovered in France by M. Daguerre, which is called by his name. M. Gouraud is the pupil and friend of the inventor, and comes to this country to make known the process. The pictures he has are extremely beautiful. They consist of views in Paris and exquisite collections of the objects of still life. The manner of producing them constitutes one of the wonders of modern times, and like other miracles, one may almost be excused for disbelieving it without seeing the very process by which it is created. It appears to me a confusion of the very elements of nature. It is nothing less than the palpable effect of light occasioning a reproduction of sensible objects. The reflection of surrounding images created by a camera, obscured upon a plate of copper, plated with silver, and prepared with some chemical substances, is not only distinctly delineated, but left upon the plate so prepared and there remains forever. Every object, however minute, is a perfect transcript of the thing itself; the hair of the human head, the gravel of the roadside, the texture of a silk curtain, or the shadow of the smaller leaf reflected upon the wall, are all imprinted as carefully as nature or art has created them in the objects transferred; and those things which are invisible to the naked eye are rendered apparent by the help of a magnifying glass. . . . How greatly ashamed of their ignorance the by-gone generations of mankind ought to be!

DECEMBER 5, THURSDAY

A most outrageous revolt has broken out among the tenants of the late patroon, Gen. Van Rensselaer, in the neighborhood of Albany, of a piece with the vile disorganizing spirit which overspreads the land like a cloud and daily increases in darkness. The tenants of the manor of Rensselaer, which is in extent from 20 to 40 miles, having waited for the decease of their respected proprietor, the late patroon, have now risen *en masse*, and refuse to pay their rents to his son Stephen, to whom that portion of the estate of his father has been bequeathed, except upon their own terms and at their own good pleasure. They have enjoyed their leases for so many years, upon terms so easy, and have been treated with so much lenity, that they have brought themselves to believe that the lands belonged to them. Since the death of Gen. Van Rensselaer they have had meetings and resolved that in a land of liberty there is no liberty for landlords,

OVERLEAF: **M. B. Brady's New Photographic Gallery, Corner of Broadway and Tenth Street, New York. The invention of photography had been announced, in Paris, only a few months prior to Hone's visit with Daguerre's agent to see "one of the wonders of modern times." Mathew Brady, who started out as a lithographer, became a daguerreotypist about 1842, with his first studio on Broadway just opposite Barnum's Museum.** (*Frank Leslie's Illustrated Newspaper*)

*Trinity Church, Wall Street,
View West from Broad,* painting,
1820. The second Trinity Church
on that site, it was demolished in
1839 to make way for a third edifice. (NYHS)

that no man has a right to own more land than his neighbors, and that they have paid so little rent heretofore that it is not worth while to pay any hereafter; and that Master Stephen, with as good a title by inheritance as any known to the laws of the State, shall neither have his land nor the income of it.

This outrageous proceeding of the Rensselaerwickers has occasioned great consternation in Albany. The sheriff resorted to the ancient process of summoning the *posse comitatus*; the citizens were ordered put to march against the rioters; several hundreds went, and met the enemy in the disputed territory. The sheriff, with seventy followers, went forward in advance; but finding them armed and mounted to the number of several thousands, determined to resist, and swearing by Dunder and Plitzen that they would pay no more, nor surrender their farms to the rightful owner, he returned to the main body of his forces, faced to the right about, and marched back to Albany.

DECEMBER 10, TUESDAY

In removing the foundations of the tower of Trinity Church a vaulted grave was opened, which contained the coffin and bones of Lady Cornbury, wife of the governor of the colony, who died in this city in the year 1706, and was buried under the original church, which was burned in the time of the Revolutionary War. A large plate and fragments of the coffin were found, which are now seen in the office of the architect; the former is perfectly legible, and nearly uninjured by its inhumation of nearly 133 years. The arms of this noble lady, who was sister of the Earl of Richmond and a viscountess in her own right, are engraven on the plate, with her pedigree, age, and time of her death, etc., distinctly, but very rudely, written below. She died at the age of thirty-four. This relic is interesting and valuable, as it marks the period of Lord Cornbury's government, one of the early English governors, whose name is affixed to the charter of Trinity Church. How many generations of men have passed away and what changes have occurred since this plate of silver emblazoned by the hands of an unskillful artist with the pompous display of heraldic pride, and the unerring record of death's doings, was placed in its dark, cold repository, to be now brought forth again to the light of day to undergo the scrutiny of a generation of men who were not thought of in those days, and who care no more about the remains of this branch of the Richmond family than of those of the poor Indian chief who was driven from the spot before her husband came to it as the representative of the majesty of England!

View of the Capitol, lithograph by
Charles Currier, c. 1840s. The
east side of the Capitol, before the
great dome was in place and surmounted by Thomas Crawford's
Statue of Freedom in the 1850s.
(MCNY)

1840

Hone, on a visit to the Capitol in Washington to attend the funeral of Commodore Isaac Chauncey, a distinguished naval figure and former commandant of the Brooklyn Navy Yard, records his vivid admiration of the golden oratory of Senator William Campbell Preston of South Carolina.

Hone's comment on the society reporter at the Henry Brevoorts' costume ball in their mansion near the corner of Ninth Street and Fifth Avenue and his reproof of the intrusive journalism of James Gordon Bennett, editor of the *New York Herald* and the Rupert Murdock of his day, mark the advent of the kind of personal reporting that has reached its zenith in our own time.

The end of the year was saddened by the death of Hone's favorite child, Mary, wife of Jones Schermerhorn. She had never enjoyed good health.

JANUARY 30, THURSDAY   WASHINGTON, D.C.

From the funeral of Commodore Chauncey, I went to the Capitol. The House has been engaged all day in fruitless discussions about the public printer. . . . But I had a high gratification in the Senate, where my good fortune carried me, and I was kept enchained until the hour of their adjournment. The whole Whig strength was brought out in opposition to the report of a special committee, of which Mr. Grundy, the later attorney-general, is chairman . . . the object of which is to show to the world the amount of the indebtedness of the several States, exaggerated in its statements and uncandid in its conclusions, charging the States with improvidence and extravagance, telling the creditor, foreign or at home, that he has trusted too much, and it is doubtful if he will be paid; and, like a cruel step-mother, the government seeking to discredit her own children and discourage their future exertions.

But what a burst of eloquence was poured from our side of the Senate upon the heads of these unworthy forgers of lies; these tinkers of government jobs; these false lights of a misguided people! Speeches were made by Crittenden, Southard, Webster, and Preston. What a host! There never was a time in the British Parliament when four such men made speeches upon one subject. They were all great, but I was most pleased with Mr. Preston. It was the first time I had ever heard the eloquent South Carolinian. He is a tall man, of a strongly marked expression of countenance and not very graceful manner; but he pours forth a flood of eloquence like a mountain cataract—broad and impetuous at one time, and clear and sweet and beautiful at another; flowing deep and solemn

OVERLEAF: *Capitol Building, Washington, D.C.*, daguerreotype by John Plumbe, 1845-46. The west side of the Capitol, as it appeared during Hone's visits. (LC)

now, and again breaking into myriads of shining particles, illuminated by the sunlight of a poetical imagination, and reflecting the varied hues of classical imagery; solemn and playful, argumentative and satirical, by turns. His voice is powerful, with occasional touches of surpassing sweetness; and then, in private intercourse, he is so playful, his conversation is so varied, and his spirits so buoyant, that I am of the opinion at this moment that I have never met a more lovable man. I sat near Mr. Preston on the floor of the Senate whilst he was speaking. He came to me after he had concluded. "There!" said he; "I made that speech on purpose for you. I had no idea that you should go home without showing you what I could do."

I am curious to know what the colleague of this noble gentleman—what Mr. [John C.] Calhoun thought of his position. . . . My eye glanced from the towering height from which one of these men launched the thunder of his eloquence upon the unworthy associate of the other, to the opposite place, where I saw the dark, scowling aspect of disappointed ambition and fallen greatness.

John C. Calhoun, **engraving from a Mathew Brady photograph. (LC)**

FEBRUARY 28, FRIDAY   NEW YORK CITY

The great affair which has occupied the minds of the people of all stations, ranks, and employments, from the fashionable belle who prepared for conquest to the humble *artiste* who made honestly a few welcome dollars in providing the weapons; from the liberal-minded gentleman who could discover no crime in an innocent and refined amusement of this kind to the newspaper reformer striving to sow the seeds of discontentment in an unruly population—this long-anticipated affair came off last evening, and I believe the expectations of all were realized. The mansion of our entertainers, Mr. and Mrs. Brevoort, is better calculated for such a display than any other in the city, and everything which host and hostess could do in preparing and arranging, in receiving their guests and making them feel a full warrant and assurance of welcome, was done to the topmost round of elegant hospitality. Mrs. B. in particular, by her kind and courteous deportment, threw a charm over the splendid pageant which would have been incomplete without it.

My family contributed a large number of actors in the gay scene. I went as Cardinal Wolseley, in a grand robe of new scarlet merino, with an exceedingly well-contrived cap of the same material; a cape of real ermine, which I borrowed from Mrs. Thomas W. Ludlow, gold chain and cross, scarlet stockings, etc.; Mary and Catharine as Day and Night; Margaret, Annot Lyle in "The Legend of Montrose"; John as Washington Irving's royal poet; Schermerhorn as Gessler, the Austrian governor who helped make William Tell immortal; Robert a Highlander, and our sweet neighbor Eliza Russell as Lalla Rookh. We had a great preparatory gathering of friends to see our dresses and those of several others, who took us "in their way up." I am not quite sure whether the pleasantest part of such an affair does not consist in "the note of preparation," the contriving and fixing . . . ; and perhaps, after all is over, the greatest doubt is *si le jeu vaut la chandelle*.

And if ever that question is tested, it must be by this experiment, for never before has New York witnessed a fancy ball so splendidly gotten up, in better taste, or more successfully carried through. We went at ten o'clock, at which time the numerous apartments, brilliantly lighted, were tolerably well filled with characters. The notice on the cards of invitation, *costume à la rigueur*, had virtually closed the door to all others, and with the exception of some eight or ten gentlemen who, in plain dress with a red ribbon at the buttonhole, officiated as managers, every one appeared as some one else; the dresses being generally new, some of them superbly ornamented with gold, silver, and jewelry;

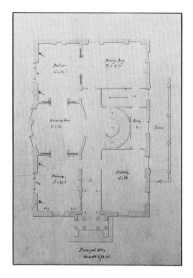

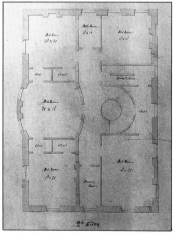

OPPOSITE and ABOVE: Elevation and plans of the Henry Brevoort House, by Alexander Jackson Davis. Hone attended a masquerade ball at the Brevoort mansion and judged it "better calculated for such a display than any other in the city." (MCNY)

others marked by classical elegance, or appropriately designating distinguished characters of ancient and modern history and the drama; and others again most familiarly grotesque and ridiculous. The *coup d'oeil* dazzled the eyes and bewildered the imagination.

Soon after our party arrived the five rooms on the first floor (including the library) were completely filled. I should think there were about 500 ladies and gentlemen. Many a beautiful "point device," which had cost the fair or gallant wearer infinite pains in the selection and adaptation, was doomed to pass unnoticed in the crowd; and many who went there hoping each to be the star of the evening, found themselves eclipsed by some superior luminary, or at best forming a unit in the milky way. Some surprise was expressed at seeing in the crowd a man in the habit of a knight in armor—a Mr. Attree, reporter and one of the editors of an infamous penny paper called the *Herald.* Bennett, the principal editor, called upon Mr. Brevoort to obtain permission for this person to be present to report in his paper an account of the ball. He consented, as I believe I should have done in the same circumstances, as by doing so a sort of obligation was imposed upon him to refrain from abusing the house, the people of the house, and their guests, which would have been done in case of a denial. But this is a hard alternative to submit to. This kind of surveillance is getting to be intolerable, and nothing but the force of public opinion will correct the insolence, which, it is to be feared, will never be applied as long as Mr. Charles A. Davis and other gentlemen make this Mr. Attree "hail fellow well met," as they did on this occasion. Whether the notice which they took of him, and that which they extend to Bennett when he shows his ugly face in Wall Street, may be considered approbatory of the daily slanders and unblushing impudence of the paper they conduct, or is intended to purchase their forbearance toward themselves, the effect is equally mischievous. It affords them countenances and encouragement, and they find that the more personalities they have in their paper the more papers they sell.

24 Fifth Avenue

In Memoriam, lithograph by Nathaniel Currier, 1846. A family mourns the death of a loved one in the cemetery of St. Paul's Chapel, a few doors down from Hone's home. (MCNY)

November 16, Monday

There is a chasm of three days in this journal, and gracious Heaven, how has the time been filled! My strength fails me when I attempt to account for it, and yet I feel that it will afford me a sort of melancholy consolation. My heart sinks within me, whenever my thoughts are concentrated on the greatest grief which has ever oppressed it. May the indulgent Father of Mercies sustain me and my bereaved family in this great hour of my affliction, and teach us with resignation to exclaim, "Father, thy will be done!" My dear, beloved Mary left this world of trouble and affliction, and as I firmly and confidently believe, joined her sister angels in Heaven, on Friday morning at half past six o'clock. Long and severe as her illness has been, and great as her sufferings, at times she has appeared to be so much better that the blessed rays of hope have shone round her, and we have indulged the delusive expectation that the cherished flower would be reanimated and bloom once more in its former loveliness.

Friday was a melancholy day. The body was deposited in its coffin, and placed in the back parlor. After the family had all gone to bed, I obtained the key of the room and taking a lamp went into the chamber of death, seated myself at the side of the cold remains of my darling child, and for half an hour held in imagination delightful converse with the spirit which had of late animated it. The countenance was unchanged, the expression intelligent and lovely as it was wont to be, and that smile, sweet as the smile of a seraph, still hung upon her half-closed lips, and I gazed with fixed eyes upon it, until I almost fancied it moved and spoke to me again. It is strange that I could derive consolation from looking upon the wreck of that which my heart held so dear, and yet it was a half hour of delightful enjoyment. Never shall I desire to have it effaced from my remembrance.

1841

Hone notes the opening of the rotunda of the new Merchants' Exchange in Wall Street. This edifice, now occupied by Citicorp at 55 Wall Street, is one of the greatest of the city's landmarks. The gold dome has been covered over by higher stories and a second elevation of columns designed by McKim, Mead & White, but the interior can still be viewed from the main hall below.

Martin Van Buren, on whom Hone called on February 19, was then a lame duck president, since William Henry Harrison, the Whig candidate who had defeated him overwhelmingly, was not inaugurated until March 4. President Harrison died of pneumonia on April 4.

FEBRUARY 19, FRIDAY   WASHINGTON, D.C.

I called this morning upon President Van Buren. He received me alone in his study, in the kindest and most gracious manner; talked a little about the late political contest, professed an undiminished friendship for me, notwithstanding my opposition, which, he said he had been gratified to learn, had been unaccompanied by the use of any expression of personal disrespect. He is fat and jolly, with the same self-satisfied smile upon his countenance. A stranger would be greatly at a loss to discover anything to indicate that he was a defeated candidate for the high office which he is about to vacate.

The Supreme Court was for two hours the point of superior attraction. Mr. [Daniel] Webster was engaged in one of those great arguments on a Constitutional question in which he stands unrivaled, the interest of which was enhanced from its being one of the last in which he will be engaged. He has resigned his seat in the Senate, from which he will take leave on Monday, and on the fourth of March he commences a new sphere of action as Secretary of State in Gen. Harrison's Cabinet.

The Supreme Court presented a sublime and beautiful spectacle during Mr. Webster's argument. The solemn temple of justice was filled with an admiring auditory consisting of a large proportion of well-dressed ladies who occupied the seats within the bar. The nine judges in their magisterial robes, attentive and thoughtful; and all minds and bodies bent upon one great object, and that object a single man, of commanding presence and intellectual aspect, not remarkably correct in his costume, nor graceful in his action, but commanding by the force of his giant intellect and irresistible control over the minds of all who heard him, and enchaining all their faculties to one point of observation and attention.

OPPOSITE: A political banner for Martin Van Buren's final presidential campaign, lithograph by Nathaniel Currier, 1848. When Hone called on him in 1841, Van Buren was a lame duck president, having lost to William Henry Harrison. He tried again in 1848, but lost to Zachary Taylor. (MCNY)

SEPTEMBER 23, THURSDAY   NEW YORK CITY

Having received from the president and directors of the New York and Erie Railroad Company an invitation to attend the ceremony of the opening of the first section of the road from Piermont on the North River through the county of Rockland to Goshen, Orange County, I was one of the 450 guests who assembled yesterday morning on board the steamboat *Utica* and started on our excursion at eight o'clock. Such a crowd of important and distinguished men, official and unofficial, I have seldom or never seen collected. An accident like that of the *Lexington* on the Sound, or the *Erie* on Lake Erie, would have vacated more offices, broken up more establishments, and broken more hearts than a seven years' war or a general conflagration of the city. We had the Governor, judges of all grades, bishop and other clergymen, mayor, recorder, members of the common council, ex-mayors, merchants, bankers, generals . . . ; and thus huddled together with scarcely standing room on the deck of the steamer, we arrived at the company's pier at Piermont, 25 miles from New York, were stowed away as close as Locofoco matches in a box (but happily not rendered equally combustible by attraction) into the cars prepared for the occasion, some of which were temporary platforms with seats of rough plank calculated for 100 persons each, and exposed to a constant shower of sparks and cinders like those which accompany a visit to Vesuvius or Etna, only not half so romantic and worthy to be talked and written about. Thus placed and *toted* by two whizzing, snorting, fire-and-smoke vomiting locomotives, we set off under the discharge of cannon, the hurrahs in English and Irish of the men, and the occasional waving of handkerchiefs (when they had them) by the women, by which we were also saluted on the whole line of the road. We went on rather slowly to be sure, but fast enough for so great a weight on a new and untried road, and arrived at Goshen, 46 miles, at two o'clock. Here the cannon were firing, bells ringing, and such a collection of people from the adjacent country as were probably never before assembled in the "land of Goshen."

OPPOSITE: *Awful Conflagration of the Steamboat Lexington in Long Island Sound,* **lithograph by Nathaniel Currier, 1840. The Lexington was built in 1835 by Cornelius Vanderbilt, and it was the best-loved of all Long Island Sound steamboats serving the favorite passenger route between New York and Boston. Only four out of 150 passengers survived the disaster. (Heritage Plantation of Sandwich, Mass.)**

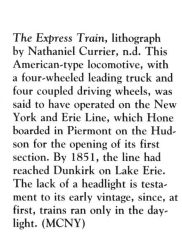

The Express Train, lithograph by Nathaniel Currier, n.d. This American-type locomotive, with a four-wheeled leading truck and four coupled driving wheels, was said to have operated on the New York and Erie Line, which Hone boarded in Piermont on the Hudson for the opening of its first section. By 1851, the line had reached Dunkirk on Lake Erie. The lack of a headlight is testament to its early vintage, since, at first, trains ran only in the daylight. (MCNY)

NOVEMBER 17, WEDNESDAY

The rotunda of the Merchants' Exchange in Wall Street, the magnificent room in which the merchants of New York are to "congregate," was opened this day for their use. The façade wants three columns to be complete, and the offices are all occupied by brokers, banks, money-changers, and those who deal in *pigeons* if not "those who sell doves." The following memoranda are taken from the account in one of the morning papers of this superb edifice, which will be an ornament to the city, but a very bad concern for the stockholders, of which number I am one to the amount of $2,500. I may say as Gomerts, the Philadelphia Jew, said to me when I congratulated him on the news of peace: "Thank you, thank you, Mr. Hone, but I wish I had not bought them calicoes."

The Merchants' Exchange Company was incorporated in 1823 or thereabouts with a capital of a million; the building with the ground cost $250,000. This building was burnt down in the great fire of 1835. The present building occupies the whole block of which the old one formed a part. It is 198 feet on Wall Street, 140 feet 8 inches on Hanover Street, and 190 feet on William Street. The center of the edifice is to be occupied as the Exchange. It is in the form of a rotunda, 80 feet in diameter in the clear. . . . The ground on which the building stands cost $750,000. The cost of the building will be about $1,100,000, so that the whole expense will not be much short of two millions, and it is doubted whether the revenue of all kinds . . . will be more than sufficient to pay the interest on the foreign debt contracted over and above the amount of subscriptions raised from such simpletons as myself for the erection of this costly temple of mercantile pride.

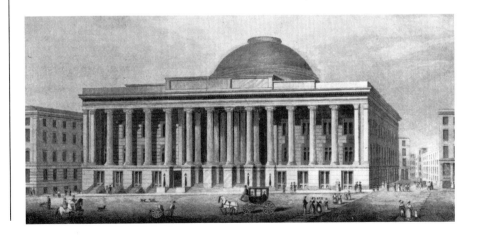

OPPOSITE: The rotunda of the new Merchants' Exchange and its facade (at right). Hone was an unhappy investor in this building. (MCNY)

1842

Charles Dickens, idolized on both sides of the Atlantic, was later bitterly to disappoint his admirer Hone with his sharp comments on the United States in his *American Notes.*

FEBRUARY 15, TUESDAY

The agony is over; the Boz ball, the greatest affair in modern times, the tallest compliment ever paid a little man, the fullest libation ever poured upon the altar of the muses, came off last evening in fine style. Everything answered the public expectation, and no untoward circumstance occurred to make anybody sorry he went.

The theater was prepared for the occasion with great splendor and taste. The whole area of the stage and pit was floored over and formed an immense saloon. The decorations and paintings were all "Pickwickian." Shields with scenes painted from the several stories of Dickens, the titles of his works on others surrounded with wreaths, the dome formed of flags, and the side walls in fresco, representing the panels of an ancient oaken hall. A small stage was erected at the extreme end opposite the main entrance, before which a curtain was suspended, exhibiting the portly proportions of the immortal Pickwick, his prince of valets, and his bodyguard of choice cronies. This curtain was raised in the intervals between the cotillions and waltzes to disclose a stage on which were exhibited a series of *tableaux vivants,* forming groups of the characters in the most striking incidents of "Pickwick," "Nicholas Nickleby," "Oliver Twist," "The Old Curiosity Shop," "Barnaby Rudge," etc. The company began to assemble at half past seven o'clock, and at nine, when the committee introduced Mr. and Mrs. Dickens, the crowd was immense; a little upward of two thousand tickets were handed in at the door, and, with the members of committees and their parties who came in by back ways, the assembled multitude numbered about two thousand five hundred. Everybody was there, and every lady was dressed well and in good taste, and decorum and good order were preserved during the whole evening. Refreshments were provided in the saloons on the several floors, and in the green room, which was kept for the members of the committees and their families. This branch of the business was farmed out to Downing, the great man of oysters, who received $2,200. On the arrival of the "observed of all observers," a lane was opened through the crowd, through which he and his lady were marched to the upper end, where the committee of reception were stationed. Here I, as chairman of the committee, received him, and made a short speech, after which they joined in the dancing. Everything went off well except the arrangement for receiving coats, hats, etc., which by the time I came away were all "in pie," as the printers say of their types, and I was fain to make my way home as best I could, without coat or hat. I went this morning and got the former, but the hat is "no more office of mine." The scene in the box office was amusing; there was a pyramid of integuments which had, like mine, been abandoned in despair, large enough to form the stock in trade of a clothing store—hats, cloaks, coats, ladies' shawls, caps, and overshoes, waiting to be claimed by such persons as had not gotten better ones in their stead.

The author of the "Pickwick Papers" is a small, bright-eyed, intelligent-looking young fellow, thirty years of age, somewhat of a dandy in his dress, with "rings and things and fine array," brisk in his manner and of a lively conversation. If he does not get his little head turned by all this, I shall wonder at it. Mrs. Dickens is a little, fat, English-looking woman, of an agreeable countenance, and, I should think, a "nice person."

Charles Dickens, carte-de-visite photograph in his later years. Hone was committee chairman for the Boz Ball given in honor of this literary lion. (MCNY)

1844

Richard M. Blatchford, a millionaire lawyer at whose splendid villa at Hell Gate Hone frequently dined, was a member of the Hone Club. He married Hone's daughter Margaret after the death of the diarist.

John Jacob Astor, a native of Germany, had emigrated to America in 1784 to become the richest man in the country of his adoption and the founder of a family famous in England as well as the United States.

OCTOBER 9, WEDNESDAY

I went out yesterday to dine at Mr. Blatchford's, at Hell Gate. The party at dinner consisted of old Mr. John Jacob Astor and his train-bearer and prime minister, Mr. Coggeswell; Mr. Jaudon; Ole Bull, the celebrated Norwegian violinst (we used to call it fiddler); and myself. In the evening the party was increased by the addition of Mr. [Daniel] Webster, his brother-in-law Mr. Page, and Mr. and Mrs. Curtis. Ole Bull had his two violins, and astonished and pleased us by his wonderful performance. Every note was sounded, from the roaring of a lion to the whisper of a summer evening's breeze; every instrument of music seemed to send forth its peculiar tones.

After an hour or two passed in the billiard room I retired to bed. When I arose this morning at Mr. Blatchford's I contemplated the delightful scene: the clumps of fine old trees clothed in the gorgeous foliage of autumn, the lawn

This view of Hell Gate, at the top of Manhattan Island, comes from a 1778 issue of *London Magazine.* (MCNY)

still bright and green, the mild, refreshing breeze, the rapid waters of Hell Gate covered with sailing vessels and steamboats—all combined to present a picture of consummate beauty. In this place, so rich in the beauties of art and nature, in the enjoyment of pecuniary independence and happy in his family relations, did the former occupant commit suicide! I slept in the room in which Mr. Prime committed the fatal act.

Mr. Astor, one of our dinner companions yesterday, presented a painful example of the insufficiency of wealth to prolong the life of man. This old gentleman with his fifteen millions of dollars would give it all to have my strength and physical ability, and yet with this example and that recorded above, I, with a good conscience and in possession of my bodily faculties, sometimes repine at my lot. He would pay all my debts if I could ensure him one year of my health and strength, but nothing else would extort so much from him. His life has been spent in amassing money, and he loves it as much as ever. He sat at the dinner table with his head down upon his breast, saying very little, and in a voice almost unintelligible; the saliva dropping from his mouth, and a servant behind him to guide the victuals which he was eating, and to watch him as an infant is watched. His mind is good, his observation acute, and he seems to know everything that is going on. But the machinery is all broken up, and there are some people, no doubt, who think he has lived long enough.

John Jacob Astor, engraving. At the time Hone dined with the old fur trader, a few years before his death, he was the richest man in America. (MCNY)

1845

MARCH 29, SATURDAY

Old men are apt to be careless and slovenly in their dress—that is wrong. Our excellent friend Chancellor Kent is eighty-two years of age, yet he is particular in his dress, and his clothes are made in good taste by a fashionable tailor. Great men, statesmen, divines, eminent lawyers, physicians, and magistrates should dress well. It gives them consideration and raises their several professions in the eyes of their fellow men; black is safest—it is peculiarly the garb of a gentleman, and never goes out of style. But in this matter of dress one of our great men (than whom there is none greater), Mr. Webster, has a strange fancy. He is not slovenly, but on the contrary tawdry, fond of a variety of colors. I do not remember ever to have seen him in the only dress in which he should appear—the respectable and dignified suit of black. I was much amused a day or two since by meeting him in Wall Street, at high noon, in a bright blue satin vest, sprigged with gold flowers, a costume as incongruous for Daniel Webster as ostrich feathers for a sister of charity.

1846

OPPOSITE: *Gen'l. Tom Thumb's Marriage at Grace Church, N.Y., Feby. 10th 1863*, lithograph by Currier & Ives, 1863. (MCNY)

JUNE 17, TUESDAY

The universal American nation is in mourning [for the death of Andrew Jackson]. Stripes, black as those which border certain resolutions in the archives of the Senate, darken the columns of the newspapers. The flags on vessels' masts, liberty poles, and public houses are hoisted at half mast; the conscript fathers of the city, overwhelmed with grief, suspend their labors and retire, sorrowing, to their respective domiciles; the standard of the Empire Club is shrouded in crêpe, and the newspaper boys blow their horns and proclaim the news of Gen. Jackson's death. Now, to my thinking, the country had greater cause to mourn on the day of his birth than on that of his decease.

Grace Church was designed by James Renwick, who later designed Saint Patrick's Cathedral. Hone rightly predicts that it will become the most fashionable church in town. A society wedding there in the 1870s is vividly described in Edith Wharton's novel, *The Age of Innocence*. Tom Thumb, P. T. Barnum's celebrated midget, was also married there, in 1863, and the *New York Times* described the guests as "the elite, the creme de la creme, the upper ten, the bonton, the select few, the very FF's of the City, nay of the Country." Earlier that year, Hone had taken his daughter Margaret to the American Museum "to see the greatest little mortal who has ever been exhibited." He described him as "a handsome, well-formed and well-proportioned little gentleman, lively, agreeable, sprightly and talkative."

FEBRUARY 5, THURSDAY

The new church at the head of Broadway is nearly finished and ready for consecration. The pews were sold last week and brought extravagant prices, some $1200 to $1400, with a pew rent on the estimated value of eight per cent; so that the word of God, as it came down to us from fishermen and mechanics, will cost the quality who worship in this splendid temple about three dollars every Sunday. This may have a good effect; for many of them,

though rich, know how to calculate, and if they do not go regularly to church they will not get the worth of their money.

This is to be the fashionable church, and already its aisles are filled (especially on Sundays after the morning services in other churches) with gay parties of ladies in feathers and *mousseline-de-laine* dresses, and dandies with mustaches and high-heeled boots; the lofty arches resound with astute criticisms upon *Gothic architecture* from fair ladies who have had the advantages of foreign travel, and scientific remarks upon acoustics from elderly millionaires who do not hear quite so well as formerly. The church is built of white marble, in the extreme of the florid Gothic, in the form of a cross. The exterior is beautiful, and its position at the commencement of the bend of Broadway, which brings it directly in view from below, striking and prominent.

OCTOBER 27, TUESDAY

I witnessed this morning, from the steps of Clinton Hall, a scene which is calculated to cause alarm as to future collisions between the citizens of this country,—a trifling incident in the appalling drama which we shall be called to witness, and perhaps bear a part in, during the course of not many years. A negro boy, named George Kirk, a slave from Georgia, secreted himself in a vessel commanded by Captain Buckley, and was brought to New York. Here he was arrested and confined, at the instance of the captain, who is subjected to severe penalties for the abduction of the slave. The claim of the master to have the fugitive sent back to Georgia was tried before Judge Edwards; N. B. Blunt appearing for the captain, and Mr. John Jay and J. L. White for the slave.

The judge's decision set the boy free, for want of evidence to prove his identity; and such a mob, of all colours, from dirty white to shining black, came rushing down Nassau and into Beekman Street as made peaceable people shrink into places of security. Such shouting and jostling, such peals of negro triumph, such uncovering of woolly heads in raising the greasy hats to give effect to the loud huzzas of the sons of Africa, seemed almost to "fright the neighborhood from its propriety." A carriage was brought to convey the hero of the day from his place of concealment, but it went away without him. This is all very pretty; but how will it end? How long will the North and the South remain a united people?

1847

The sculpture, *The Greek Slave* by Hiram Powers, that Hone so admired on September 13, was the first life-size statue of a nude female on public display in America. Exhibited in 1851 at London's Crystal Palace, it returned to America in 1853 for New York's Crystal Palace, where it caused a sensation.

The Greek Slave by Hiram Powers, 1847. Hone viewed this marble sculpture at the National Academy several years before it caused a sensation at New York's Crystal Palace, 1853-54, as the first life-size statue of a nude female publicly exhibited. (Brooklyn Museum)

January 29, Friday

Our good city of New York has already arrived at the state of society to be found in the large cities of Europe; overburdened with population, and where the two extremes of costly luxury in living, expensive establishments, and improvident waste are presented in daily and hourly contrast with squalid misery and hopeless destitution. This state of things has been hastened in our case by the constant stream of European paupers arriving upon the shores of this land of promise. Alas! how often does it prove to the deluded emigrant a land of broken promise and blasted hope! If we had none but our own poor to take care of, we should get along tolerably well; we could find employment for them, and individual charity, aiding the public institutions, might save us from the sights of woe with which we are assailed in the streets, and the pressing applications which beset us in the retirement of our own houses. Nineteen out of twenty of these mendicants are foreigners cast upon our shores, indigent and helpless, having expended the last shilling in paying their passage-money, deceived by the misrepresentations of unscrupulous agents, and left to starve amongst strangers, who, finding it impossible to extend relief to all, are deterred from assisting any. These reflections upon the extremes of lavish expenditure and absolute destitution are forced upon me by my own recent experience. I partook yesterday of a most expensive dinner, where every article of costly food which the market affords was spread before the guests, and fine wines drunk in abundance, some of which might command eight or ten dollars a bottle; and from this scene of expensive hospitality I was conveyed to another more splendid and expensive entertainment, where the sparkling of diamonds, the reflection of splendid mirrors, the luster of silks and satins, the rich gilding of tasteful furniture were flashed, by the aid of innumerable lights, upon the dazzled eyes of a thousand guests. Now this is all right enough; in both these cases our entertainers could well afford the expense which attended the display of their hospitality, nor is it within the scope of the most remote probability that the money of any others than themselves can be involved in the outlay of their entertainments.

SEPTEMBER 13

A beautiful piece of statuary [*The Greek Slave*], the work of Hiram Powers, the celebrated American sculptor at Rome, is now being exhibited at the National Academy, and attracts crowds of visitors from morning to night. And so it ought, for it is admirable. I have no rule by which to estimate the merit, or appreciate the faultless beauty, of this statue which could guide me in placing it below the Venus de Medici. I have no personal acquaintance with Powers, nor had I with Praxiteles; but I am not willing to undervalue my countryman because he was not born so soon as the other gentlemen of the chisel. I certainly never saw anything more lovely.

The National Academy of Design, engraving, 1865. Founded in 1826 to further the cause of American art, the Academy moved into this new building at the corner of Fourth Avenue and 23rd Street in 1865. (*Frank Leslie's Illustrated Newspaper*)

1848

The four paintings of Thomas Cole in the series entitled "The March of Empire" are now in The New-York Historical Society, where also are to be found the manuscripts of Hone's and George Templeton Strong's diaries. Hone had described the fortieth anniversary of this institution, of which he was a vice-president, in 1844, "where an address was delivered by Mr. Broadhead, the gentleman who was sent out by the state to collect from the archives of Europe annals and records and documents relating to the history of the United States, and especially such as concerned the settlement and early history of New York."

FEBRUARY 15

Died on Saturday, the 12th, at his residence, Kattskill, Thomas Cole. The death of this eminent artist, in the prime of life and the meridian of his fame as a landscape painter, is a loss to the arts and a severe affliction to his friends, for both suffer equally from the melancholy deprivation. I knew poor Cole from the first day he came here from Philadelphia,—a fine young fellow, full of undying ardor in the pursuit of knowledge, a lover of nature, with a conscious ability for the portraiture of her features. Modest and unassuming, he was unacquainted with the artistical quality of humbug, and, alas! he was not then the fashion. If genius did not sometimes overcome discouragement, here was a case in which it might have despaired. When Cole came to New York he brought with him two pictures, original views of the *Kaaters Kill* or Kattskill mountains, and the Still-Lake which forms its head-waters, with all the beautiful scenery of that romantic region, taken on the spot. Days were devoted to rambling, sketching, and the results successfully transferred to the canvas: the glowing impressions of a warm imagination, the rich fruits of an artist's study, the children of prolific genius; and these pictures, the labor of many weary days taken faithfully and with talent from one of the most beautiful repositories of nature's riches, the artist offered for sale repeatedly, in Philadelphia, for ten dollars each, without finding a purchaser; for he was not then the fashion. These pictures are now mine; they adorn the wall of my back parlor.

Cole came here, poor, friendless, and, worse than all, modest. He was fortunate enough, however, to attract the notice of Colonel Trumbull and William Dunlap, two artists, now both deceased, whose favorable opinion was of great value, and was freely bestowed. They bought, each of them, one of the pictures in question for $25. I was so much pleased with them that I suc-

Destruction, **painting by Thomas Cole, from his series "March of Empire," now in the New-York Historical Society. (NYHS)**

ceeded in getting the two for $125, and now that my friend, whose recent death is so deeply deplored, has emerged from the clouds of neglect and shone out in all the brightness of fashionable popularity, it is not an extravagant surmise that some of the Philadelphia *dilettanti,* who could not formerly discover $10 worth of merit in these early productions of the artist, would now be glad to buy, at a cost of $600 or $800, two of the works of his pencil, of no greater merit than mine. The late Mr. Samuel Ward gave him $2,500 for a series of four beautiful pictures, called "The Guardian Angel," and the late Mr. Luman Reed, a price nearly equal for another series of four, which he styled the "March of Empire." Poor Cole! He struggled against every discouragement to reach the top of the hill, but was not long permitted to enjoy his elevated station.

1849

The riots caused by the rivalry between the Shakespearean actors William Charles Macready, an Englishman, and Edwin Forrest, an American, seem very odd to modern readers. Forrest, a bit of a demagogue, actually ran for Congress on the Locofoco ticket. The name designated a radical Democratic faction in New York that opposed conservative Tammany leadership and was derived from the "Locofoco" matches with which its members lit candles at a party meeting when the regulars had turned off the gas. Forrest seems to have been the instigator of the riots, playing on Irish anti-British feeling. Thirty-one persons were killed and a large number wounded.

MAY 8

Mr. Macready commenced an engagement last evening at the Opera-House, Astor Place, and was to have performed the part of "Macbeth," whilst his rival, Mr. Forrest, appeared in the same part at the Broadway theater. A violent animosity has existed on the part of the latter theatrical hero against his rival, growing out of some differences in England; but with no cause, that I can discover, except that one is a gentleman, and the other is a vulgar, arrogant loafer, with a pack of kindred rowdies at his heels. Of these retainers a regularly organized force was employed to raise a riot at the Opera-House and drive Mr. Macready off the stage, in which, to the disgrace of the city, the ruffians succeeded. On the appearance of the "Thane of Cawdor," he was saluted with a shower of missiles, rotten eggs, and other unsavory objects, with shouts and yells of the most abusive epithets. In the midst of this disgraceful riot the performance was suspended, the respectable part of the audience dispersed, and the vile band of *Forresters* were left in possession of the house. This cannot end here; the respectable part of our citizens will never consent to be put down by a mob raised to serve the purpose of such a fellow as Forrest. Recriminations will be resorted to, and a series of riots will have possession of the theaters of the opposing parties.

Edwin Forrest, **lithograph by
Nathaniel Currier, n.d. (MCNY)**

OPPOSITE: *Great Riot at the Astor
Place Opera House, New York,*
**lithograph by Nathaniel Currier,
1849. (MCNY)**

MAY 10

The riot at the Opera-House on Monday night was children's play compared with the disgraceful scenes which were enacted in our part of this devoted city this evening, and the melancholy loss of life to which the outrageous proceedings of the mob naturally led.

An appeal to Mr. Macready had been made by many highly respectable citizens, and published in the papers, inviting him to finish his engagement at the Opera-House, with an implied pledge that they would stand by him against the ferocious mob of Mr. Forrest's friends, who had determined that Macready should not be allowed to play, whilst at the same time their oracle was strutting, unmolested, his "hour upon the stage" of the Broadway theater. This announcement served as a firebrand in the mass of combustibles left smoldering from the riot of the former occasion. The *Forresters* perceived that their previous triumph was incomplete, and a new conspiracy was formed to accomplish effectually their nefarious designs. Inflammatory notices were posted in the upper ward, meetings were regularly organized, and bands of ruffians, gratuitously supplied with tickets by richer rascals, were sent to take possession of the theater. The police, however, were beforehand with them, and a large body of their force was posted in different parts of the house.

When Mr. Macready appeared he was assailed in the same manner as on the former occasion; but he continued on the stage and performed his part with firmness, amidst the yells and hisses of the mob. The strength of the police, and their good conduct, as well as that of the Mayor, Recorder, and other public functionaries, succeeded in preventing any serious injury to the property within doors, and many arrests were made; but the war raged with frightful violence in the adjacent streets. The mob—a dreadful one in numbers and ferocity—assailed the extension of the building, broke in the windows, and demolished some of the doors. I walked up to the corner of Astor Place, but was glad to make my escape. On my way down, opposite the New York Hotel, I met a detachment of troops, consisting of about sixty cavalry and three hundred infantry, fine-looking fellows, well armed, who marched steadily to the field of action. Another detachment went by the way of Lafayette Place. On their arrival they were assailed by the mob, pelted with stones and brickbats, and several were carried off severely wounded.

Under this provocation, with the sanction of the civil authorities, orders were given to fire. Three or four volleys were discharged; about twenty persons were killed and a large number wounded. It is to be lamented that in the number were several innocent persons, as is always the case in such affairs. A

large proportion of the mob being lookers-on, who, putting no faith in the declaration of the magistrates that the fatal order was about to be given, refused to retire, and shared the fate of the rioters. What is to be the issue of this unhappy affair cannot be surmised; the end is not yet.

May 11

I walked up this morning to the field of battle, in Astor Place. The Opera-House presents a shocking spectacle, and the adjacent buildings were smashed with bullet-holes. Mrs. Langdon's house looks as if it had withstood a siege. Groups of people were standing around, some justifying the interference of the military, but a large proportion were savage as tigers with the smell of blood.

May 12

Last night passed off intolerably quietly, owing to the measures taken by the magistrates and police. But it is consolatory to know that law and order have thus far prevailed. The city authorities have acted nobly. The whole military force was under arms all night, and a detachment of United States troops was also held in reserve. All the approaches to the Opera-House were strictly guarded, and no transit permitted. The police force, with the addition of a thousand special constables, were employed in every post of danger; and although the lesson has been dearly bought, it is of great value, inasmuch as the fact has been established that law and order can be maintained under a Republican form of government.

1850

Catharine Dunscomb Hone, the diarist's devoted spouse, died after a long illness in May. Although the marriage lasted for half a century and seems to have been a happy one, Mrs. Hone appears infrequently in the pages of the diary. She was presumably a quiet, home-loving person, for it is usually one of the daughters rather than she who accompanies Hone on his travels and to his brilliant dinner parties.

In October, Hone's great-niece, Caroline Howland, granddaughter of his brother John, was married to his old friend, Charles H. Russell. Russell, a widower of fifty-four and the father of Hone's daughter-in-law, Eliza (wife of Robert Hone), was twenty-five years older than his bride, but Hone did not deem it necessary to mention this, or that the match converted his friend into his great-nephew-in-law. The Russells were to produce, six offspring, and Eliza and Robert, who had made their home at No. 2 Great Jones Street, next to Hone's, had to find other quarters.

MAY 24, FRIDAY

My worst apprehensions are realized. The crowning blessing of my long life, the enjoyment of which the Lord has permitted to me for a period of nearly half a century of uninterrupted love, affection, and confidence, He has seen fit to resume. The most excellent partner of my fondest associations, the best of wives, the mother of my children, my comforter in affliction, the participant of my joys, the promoter of my happiness, my friend and example, died this morning at fifteen minutes past four o'clock,—died as angels live,—peaceful, serene, sensible to the last moment, free from pain, and perfectly resigned to the will of God. And there she lies, with a benignant expression which seems to impart sweetness to the flowers with which her beloved frame is decorated. Teach me, blessed Lord, to receive this chastisement with suitable resignation and submission to Thy will. Thou hast permitted me to enjoy for a long period the blessing of which Thou hast now deprived me, and I have no right to complain. Thy will be done in this as in all other dispensations of Thy Providence!

OCTOBER 30

The great affair came off last evening, at the elegant mansion of Samuel S. Howland, whose daughter Catherine [sic] was united to Mr. Charles H. Russell in the "holy bonds of Matrimony" by the Rev. Robert Howland of the Episcopal Church, the son of Mr. Gardiner G. Howland. The affair was brilliant; the company, embracing besides all the relations and connections of the two families, a great concourse of distinguished ladies and gentlemen, strangers and citizens, who witnessed the ceremony and partook of an excellent supper. Eliza and her two sweet little girls and Mrs. William H. Russell and her two lovely children were among the most interesting objects in the grand display. This marriage will make a great revolution in the affairs of No. 2 Great Jones Street. The bride and groom will sail for Europe on the 16th of the next month and on their return Robert and his concern must evacuate the premises. May happiness and prosperity be the result of this union.

NOVEMBER 16

The noble steamer [Baltic] went off magnificently, precisely at her appointed time, 12 o'clock, with the punctuality that characterizes all such things in our country. Our friend and neighbor, Mr. Charles H. Russell, his newly married wife and daughter Fanny, were passengers, and left us in tears for their departure and prayers for their safety.

1851

Philip Hone, **painting attributed to D. Huntington, perhaps the one done for the Hone Club. (NYHS)**

APRIL 30, WEDNESDAY

This volume of my journal, which has only four vacant leaves to be completed, has been suspended during nearly the whole month by continued unmitigated illness and incapacity to perform any act of mental or physical ability. Feeble beyond description, utterly destitute of appetite, with no strength in my limbs, and no flesh upon my bones, shall this journal be resumed? During this illness I have gone occasionally to my office for a short time, and performed a little *pro forma* business; but it could have been performed by deputy. To-morrow will be the first of May. Volume 29 lies ready on my desk. Shall it go on?

Epitaph. A few years ago, during a visit I made with my dear wife to the Greenwood Cemetery, I was so struck with the beauty and simplicity of the inscription on one of the monuments,—"There is rest in Heaven,"—that I was induced on my return home to extend the idea, in order, perhaps, that it might be appropriated in my own use. It was copied in the journal at the time.

Has the time come?

The weary traveler on earth's dull road,
The pilgrim fainting underneath life's load,
The stout heart struggling 'gainst the adverse wave,
And sinking, with no mortal arm to save,
Finds hope and consolation in the blest decree
Pronounced by angels' lips—"there's rest in heaven for thee."

This was the diarist's final entry; he died on May 5.

George Templeton Strong

George Templeton Strong (1820–1875) seems just the right man to have taken over the role of chronicling the manners and events of the city after Hone's death. In 1851 Strong was thirty-one and had already been keeping a diary for fifteen years. The Strongs, unlike the Hones, had a distinguished colonial ancestry (George's grandfather had been a captain in the Continental Army), but by the middle of the nineteenth century both families belonged to the same inner circle of New York society—the Astors, Schermerhorns, Stuyvesants, Lenoxes, Brevoorts, and Howlands. Strong's law practice consisted largely in drawing wills and administering estates, which kept him very much up-to-date with what was going on among the leading families. And like Hone he was an avid amateur of the arts and a collector of rare books and fine paintings. In music he was even something more, for he played the piano and organ and was a near scholar of ecclesiastical music, organizing the Church Music Association and later becoming president of the Philharmonic Society. The breadth of his interests gives a broad coverage to his diary. We meet in its pages, as in Hone's, not only the great merchants and lawyers of the day, but writers and artists. In a grand soirée, given by the Strongs in 1858, a hundred and fifty guests gathered for supper, including the painters Thomas P. Rossiter and John Frederick Kensett, "whom it's not only creditable but aesthetic and refined to have at one's parties."

Strong resembled Hone in being a man of exuberant good will. He waxes as rosily sentimental as his predecessor over the beauties of natural scenery, the nobility of great lives, the sancity of marriage (where the woman is a

OPPOSITE: *George Templeton Strong* (1820-1875), photograph. (NYHS)

1 2 3

G. T. Strong. 108 Greenwich St

Here begins My Diary for A.D. MD.CCC.XXXVII.

January – 1. – The New Year comes in cloudy, damp, & disagreeable. – Went to St Pauls morning & afternoon – Evening – went in next door. –

January 2. Cloudy & desperately cold. A good deal of snow has fallen during the night – the thermometer is about 13° and altogether, it is just about such a day as the 16th December last. – There was a great deal of call making & visitationing going on; but my father had a very convenient "bad cold" & accordingly staid at the office all the morning – & as to visiting by myself, it was a thing not to be thought of, and therefore I prudently & wisely made no visits at all. – At about eleven I started to call on Chittenden, but he was out, & so after spending an hour or so with Backus I came home again – . = As I came down Liberty St, I saw a carriage at Mr Hillyer's, & out of it came little Benjamin Strow & (I suppose) his father. – I rather fancy that there is truth in that story about G. M— – indeed, there cannot be any doubt about it – I should like to see the fiancée – she will have a curious kind of husband! –

January 3d Tuesday. Dubious between clear & cloudy – & the thermometer lower than it had been this year – 7°; Did not go out in the morning. – Arranged some of my antiques – by the by my collection has hardly received an addition for the last three months. – Afternoon bought this book – for which I gave the mortal sum of one dollar – and then after tea turned my wits to work on a composition – the subject being Spenser's "fair Queen" – I have done about half of it – & I intend to make a diapason of it – for the subject like the poem, is interminable.

January 4th Clear & very cold – Did not go out to day – Spent the morning in arranging my mineralogy Note, etc. and the evening in finishing the composition I began last night – The new table for the Library, arrived to day – & it is a very great improvement on the old one – more spacious, & more comfortable for study, in every respect. It cost $19 & is 5 ft by 3. – The last day of the Christmas holiday – I am not very sorry – I have made up my mind, that a period of leisure is pleasant only as a change, and that we soon feel inclined to desire another change, that is, back to study again – Study, unless on some very disagreeable subject, is in my opinion preferable – & the harder the study is – the more actively the mind is engaged, the greater is the positive pleasure – The terrors of hard study all vanish on a near approach – & the more irons in the fire, the better – that is as far as regards pleasure, though perhaps not, as regards profit –

Jan. 5th News arrived of another shipwreck still more, than that of the Bristol & originating from the same cause – viz. the want of a pilot. – 108 lives lost! The ship was the Mexico of Liverpool. A little snow this morning but it soon cleared. – College. Anthon wished us a happy New Year – So did McVickar with the addition of a good deal of blarney – much in his usual style. – I am glad to see that G. Anthon is well enough to come back to Coll. – he was there – & came home with me – Read my Composition – which took up 25 minutes! – afternoon – Understanding from Tucker that there was something in the weekly Herald of last Saturday about Miss Ruth Shatton & Mr Muhlenberg I went up to the Office & got it. It dont amount to much – News of another shipwreck on Long Island, this evening. –!

Jan. 6th – Clear – Spent the afternoon quotation hunting & reading Milton – after tea went t

dutiful consort), and the delights of parenthood. He differed markedly from Hone, however, in temperament. Introspective and nervous, subject to moods of melancholia despite a Dickensian sense of humor, Strong was an earnest puritan who thought little enough of his age and less of himself, but who was desperately determined to make the best of both. If his prejudices were violent, his instincts were good; he may have disliked the Irish, the English, and Southerners, but he also detested municipal corruption and colonialism, and he abhorred slavery (though not regarding it as unconstitional, which of course in that day it was not). His greatest passion seems to have been in recording everything and everyone in the pages of his voluminous diary.

Strong was born in 1820, the son of George Washington Strong and his second wife, Eliza Catherine Templeton. His father, a lawyer, founded the Wall Street firm of Strong, Bidwell & Taft, which continues to this day under the name of Cadwallader, Wickersham & Taft. George graduated from Columbia College, of which institution he would later become an active and concerned trustee, and read law in his father's office. He became a partner in 1845 and remained such until he retired in 1873 to take the comptrollership of Trinity Corporation (handling the investments and extensive real estate of that wealthy church) two years before his death.

In 1848 Strong married Ellen Ruggles, daughter of Samuel B. Ruggles, a prominent lawyer and capitalist. While the Ruggleses were not a "better" or "older" family than the Strongs, they were more noticed in society, and the young couple moved in the most fashionable circles of Manhattan and Newport. They built a goodly sized house (what George called his "palazzo") in Grammercy Park and entertained extensively.

It seems to have been a happy union, at least from the evidence of the diary, and it produced three sons: John Ruggles Strong, George Templeton Strong, Jr., known as "Templeton," and Lewis Barton Strong. John was a lawyer and an amateur cellist. He married Laura Stewart, and they had one son, George Templeton Strong III. Templeton, the diarist's second son, quarreled with his father and left home at nineteen. He studied music for seven years at the Leipzig Conservatory and became a professional composer. One of his pieces, *Die Nacht*, was played by the N.B.C. Orchestra in 1939, conducted by Arturo Toscanini. He married three times and was the father of five children: John Sintram Strong, Percy Templeton Strong, Richard Templeton Strong, George Templeton Strong, and Olivia Templeton Strong. Lewis, the diarist's third son, was a popular and social bachelor of no profession who passed his life in New York clubs and palatial Florida hotels.

OPPOSITE: **Strong's diary, part of the first page for the year 1837. (NYHS)**

ABOVE: *Ellen Ruggles Strong, pho-tograph.* (NYHS)

BELOW: *John R. Strong, left, and George T. Strong, Jr., photo-graph.* (NYHS)

Despite his happy marriage, the diarist's attitude toward women was dis-tinctly and at times unpleasantly Victorian. He tends to use the diminutive in all references to his spouse. She is "poor, little Ellen in her ignorance and simplicity," "my most imprudent little wife," "poor dear good innocent little Ellen," or his "noble little girl." Even her tasks are dwarfed; we see her "busy with her little household arrangements."

It may be worth noting, however, that if Strong was what is now known as a male chauvinist—he did not even want women admitted to the bar—he was very firm about the absolute obligation of a husband to support his wife in near luxury, no matter what the cost to his health or fortune. And this was not simply another example of what Veblen was later to call "conspicuous consumption"—the need of the male to show off his prowess by adorning his mate. Strong had little concern for the eyes of society. He wanted his "little Ellen" to have her parties and "socialities," even if it put him in bankruptcy.

I had assumed that Ellen Strong was more or less the woman George de-scribes until I came across a very different picture of her in Mary Lydig Daly's *Diary of a Union Lady,* which has this entry for December 11, 1864:

> Ellen Strong came in, painted like a wanton, at Mrs. Bancroft's, with a huge bouquet sent her by one of her little beaux, without her husband. What must he think? What can he mean by leaving her so much to herself?

This is only one of several entries about Ellen Strong and her painted face and partiality for young men. Poor George! But presumably what he never knew could not have much hurt him.

If he never knew about Ellen, he was not permitted the bliss of similar ignorance as to the goings on of Elinor Fearing Strong, the pretty and vivacious wife of his younger cousin, law partner, and closest friend, Charles. The nu-merous entries about how Strong handled the scandal of her threat to run off with a florid and mustachioed journalist and dandy named William Hurlbert seem to me to throw significant light on the domestic mores of the decade before the Civil War, yet Allen Nevins chose not to include them in his four-volume edition of the diary. When I assembled them and offered them to *Amer-ican Heritage* I ran into a similar indifference. "Why," demanded that periodical's adviser, the great Civil War expert, Bruce Catton, "would our readers, in an era of easy divorce, be interested in the difficulties of a couple bound in 'holy deadlock'?" "And why," I retorted, "in an era outlawing slavery, would they be interested in a war to abolish it?"

Hurlbert, whom Strong refers to sarcastically as "the abbé," because he had once studied for the ministry, had managed to ease his way, with glib address and dubious social credentials, through many Fifth Avenue doors and into the heart of the romantic and impressionable Elinor. Cousin "Charley" discovered this in the summer of 1857 by reading a letter that his wife had carelessly left on a table and immediately consulted his law partner and mentor, the diarist, as to what he should do. George sternly ordained an immediate separation. Elinor was to go to her uncle's while the villain was coped with by the gentlemen of the family. It was essential to guarantee that the would-be seducer should never see the erring girl again, and to obtain from him, if humanly possible, any incriminating letters.

But the villain proved obstinate. He actually had the gall to assert that his and Elinor's mutual ardor gave him rights! For a time there seemed to be a real danger that the guilty pair might abscond to Europe to embrace the wandering life of second-class watering places to which society relegated illicitly united couples. Strong's diary positively seethes as he records his dealings with this "coprophagous insect," this "gaudily colored and fetid bug":

> Next came a letter of 8 pages from the Abbe H. to *me*, as C's friend, inviting an interview and setting forth his views. Either he is insane, or he feels himself in a horribly false position and wants to cover his retreat by bullying. I replied by a dry note, refusing to recognize his *right to be a party to any settlement between C. and his wife* (!!!—incredible as it seems, that is the ground he takes—and unless that be acceded to, he has the inconceivable baseness to threaten to blow the whole affair), and telling him I'd be home at 8 tonight, if he wanted to say anything that would enable me to be of service to the lady or the gentleman.

> And then the fetid bug actually came!

> August 2. Sunday night. That man H. has been twice in this house today. Do not its walls need ceremonial purification? The glass from which some water was given this dog when he was (unless he were shamming) over-powered by agitation I have smashed. No guest of mine shall run the risk of catching his foul disease. Things look bad and black.

In the end, however, Elinor, whose passion seems to have been less strong than that of her fiery admirer, agreed to a reconciliation with her husband. It actually lasted until after the Civil War, when she left him to reside permanently in Europe. This victory, however, was not good enough for the inexorable George. It would not do simply to bring home the erring wife. Every respectable door in New York had to be permanently closed to the wretched Hurlbert.

It is interesting that many of the people of whom Strong sought assurance that they should thereafter "cut" the would-be adulterer, at first showed some degree of resistance. Society in any era is made up largely of persons who are willing to live and let live. What had Hurlbert done, after all, that many of Manhattan's most respected clubmen had not done? But society will always smother its natural tolerance once its priests have spoken. If a priest chooses to make an issue of a particular matter and to demand public obeisance to an accepted code, he cannot be denied. At least until the code has broken down, and that had not yet happened in 1857. And Strong, of course, in the New York of his day, was a kind of priest. When he demanded: "Are you willing to stand up and be counted as an 'Aye' for adultery?" the answer had to be "no." In the same way, in our own day, he might have commanded a negative answer by asking if a person was willing to condone racism. By the time Strong had completed his calls on his friends, every brownstone of upper-class Manhattan was sealed to Elinor's panting swain. It is small wonder that Hurlbert quit the city for good.

Strong's law practice was a successful one. He was largely an office attorney, but he argued at least one important case before the U.S. Supreme Court. What strikes us as remarkable, however, is the number of civic activities he managed to combine with his profession. As a trustee of Columbia College he was one of those most active in developing that institution into a great university. He was a founder of the Law School, and he even managed to badger a conservative, stuffy, classics-oriented board into creating the School of Mines. He also gave hours of his time each week to the affairs of Trinity Church, of which he was a vestryman. Always high church in his views, he took an active interest in the General Convention of the Episcopal Church and the proceedings of its House of Bishops.

But the great job of Strong's life was the Sanitary Commission. This was the organization, founded at the beginning of the Civil War by patriotic citizens to improve military hygiene, that induced President Abraham Lincoln and Secretary of War Simon Cameron to endow it with the necessary powers to take over from the fumbling War Department the care of the wounded and the inspection of camps. Strong worked as its treasurer all during the war (very much to the detriment of his law practice, the income of which was his main source of support) to raise and disburse five millions in cash (an immense sum for those days) and direct the application of huge amounts of donated material. He conferred with President Lincoln, Secretary of War Edwin M. Stanton, General George B. McClellan, and General Ulysses S. Grant and spent at least half of his time for four years in committee meetings and field missions. Few men outside the military did more for the cause of the Union.

It is also to be noted that Strong, like Hone, had been too ardent a unionist in the years leading up to the conflict to be willing to risk secession of the Southern states by advocating abolition of slavery. His attitude was that slavery, if morally abhorrent, was still legal, being tolerated by the Constitution itself, and that as the price paid for the Union it had to be accepted, so long as geographically limited. Only with the firing on Fort Sumter did he at last become dedicated to the joint causes of union and emancipation.

Much has been written by historians of the tepid attitude of New Yorkers toward the Union cause, as manifested by the large number of Copperheads, or Southern Sympathizers, among its business leaders and the rank sedition of Irish laborers. Strong's diary contains ample evidence that to oppose this there was strong patriotic feeling in all classes. He himself was a leader of the group in the Union Club that resigned in a body because of the Southern sympathies of some of the older members and formed the purer Union League Club.

The years following the war were plagued for Strong by ill health and depression. He never, by his own confession, got himself "thoroughly into harness" in the law again. The corruption of politics and business in the postwar years disgusted him. In 1875 his ailments concentrated in the enlargement of his liver, and he died at the age of fifty-five.

The
Strong
Diary

1851

The year was darkened by the financial troubles of Strong's father-in-law. Samuel B. Ruggles had been a successful investor in city real estate. One of his projects had been the planning and development of Grammercy Park as a residential area; his own house was at No. 24 East 21st Street, facing the park, and Strong's at No. 74, just off it. But Ruggles had invested too heavily in some warehouses on the Atlantic Docks in Brooklyn. Creditors pressed him hard and accusations of fraud were made, but in the end Ruggles managed to stay solvent and ultimately to recover some of his affluence.

Jenny Lind, the "Swedish Nightingale," had made her first New York appearance at Castle Garden in September of 1850, under the aegis of P. T. Barnum, who said: "Inasmuch as my name has long been associated with humbug, and the American public suspect that my capacities do not extend beyond the power to exhibit a stuffed monkey-skin or a dead mermaid, I can afford to lose fifty thousand dollars in such an enterprise as bringing to this country in the zenith of her life and celebrity, the greatest musical wonder in the world. . . ." Nathaniel Currier issued six portraits of Jenny Lind, which are undoubtedly those Strong comments on.

October 20 saw the birth of Strong's first child, John Ruggles Strong.

MAY 5

Philip Hone (senior) died this morning; a short illness, but he has been very sadly broken down for some months. . . .

Half the city is being pulled down. The north corner of Wall and Broadway, an old landmark, is falling amid the execrations of pedestrians whom its ruins and rubbish drive off the sidewalk. The building on the north side of Trinity churchyard is to follow.

OPPOSITE: *Upper and Lower Bay of New York*, lithograph by Currier & Ives, n.d. Castle Garden, at center, was originally an old fort reached by a causeway. Gradually joined to the island by landfill, at mid-century Castle Garden was a popular concert hall. (MCNY)

MAY 12

Spent an hour trying to get myself phototyped for the benefit of my mother, but without success. . . . To No. 24 for Ellen, and a long talk with Mr. Ruggles. Things look worse; the only thing to be hoped for is euthanasia—a noiseless finale, without scandal. Life cannot be sustained—the stimulants have ceased to work—indeed, I could have predicted the result years ago if I had known the workings of the system. I don't think it desirable that it should go on.

MAY 13

For the last two hours with Mr. Ruggles. Worse and worse. He will bring down others, I fear, in his fall. H. & H. are likely to be heavy losers. It will be well if they're not ruined. F. Griffin can survive his loss, but these men and some others of the same sort will have hard work to stagger under theirs, and I fear will fall. It's a cruel business on both sides. The trust estate of Mrs. Ruggles is in a bad position, but with promptitude and good luck, I hope it may be saved from serious loss.

MAY 16, FRIDAY NIGHT

I have not been very fruitful of good works for the past three days. Mr. Ruggles's perplexities and troubles have occupied my mind a good deal and made me listless and inefficient. It is sad to see the ruinous wreck of the plans and operations that have been going on so long, the total loss of years of labor, the sacrifice of property acquired by so much energy and talent. It is sad, too, to see its effect on the domesticities of No. 24; for this will be an honest failure, to be followed up by retrenchment and close economy, and the surrender of everything but Mrs. Ruggles's private estate, or what is left of it. I could not but think of it yesterday—the change from the old, happy day of which it was the anniversary; the brightness and gaiety of the house then, and its condition now with the black shadow of insolvency at the door; the "Let us depart hence" of all its household gods; the gloom and despondency and stillness that have taken their abode in every room; John dead, Jem away, Ellie no longer there, all who remain busy in the sad work of saving the poor fragments of sudden and sickening ruin, and preparing to remove to some humbler lodging. . . .

A note will lie over at the Chemical Bank tomorrow, so the case is a pretty clear one. Mr. Ruggles tells me tonight of a matter that I'm glad of, for it breaks the fall a little; a movement on the part of W. B. Astor, the Kings, and others to raise a fund to purchase the Clarendon at its full value and a little over, and so enable him to wind up his affairs and make at least a fair settlement with his creditors. But it won't be done—it's a mere flicker of hope burning out in the socket. The case is at present perfectly remediless. May I be delivered from the lunacy of debt!

Heard Jenny Lind Wednesday night with Ellen. As much pleased as I expected to be, and no more. All that I heard her sing was overloaded with *fiorituri* and foolery, marvelously executed, but I always find that sort of thing a bore. The low and middle notes of her voice are superb, and the high notes as good as such notes can be, but she runs too much on music written for the altitudes. No doubt she does it with perfect ease, but that don't make it the pleasanter to hear. A man who could walk on his head as comfortably as on his feet would be a fatiguing person to look at, if he abused his faculty of locomotion and was habitually upside down. The lady's personal appearance took me much by surprise. None of her portraits do her any justice. She is not pretty nor handsome, nor exactly fine-looking, but there's an air about her of dignity, self-possession, modesty, and goodness that is extremely attractive.

July 17

Talk of the ennobling pursuits of literature, historic research, art, music, the elevating influence of investigations into natural science, the noble object of reviving a fit and reverent style of church architecture, and the other subjects which the better class of cultivated men select as their business or their relaxation—they are all good. But what is there for an Englishman, with more or less of surplus time and faculties, after making due provision for himself and his household, to *do* in the year of grace 1851 *before* he has done something to help the thousands and tens of thousands that are perishing hopelessly in profligacy, drunkenness, and starvation in the cellars and workshops of every city in England? It strikes me that most "liberal pursuits," no matter how purifying to the tastes and invigorating to the intellect, are something like a wretched waste of time and perversion of talent and an insane misapplication

First Appearance of Jenny Lind in America, lithograph by Nathaniel Currier, 1850. Strong wrote that he was as pleased with her singing as he "expected to be, and no more." P. T. Barnum, the impresario of this concert, is said to be the large figure standing at the side of the stage. (MCNY)

137

New York by Gas-Light, Hooking a Victim, lithograph by Serrell & Perkins, c. 1850. Strong speaks of encountering "crews" of young girls "with thief written in their cunning eyes and whore on their deprived faces." (MCNY)

of energy and industry, while men and women and children in multiplying thousands lie rotting alive, body and soul at once, in those awful catacombs of disease and crime, and even the question how to save them is yet unsolved.

And the same question is to be asked, and must be answered, here in New York; though, Heaven be praised, it does not *yet* stand out with such terrible prominence before all other questions of duty to society here as in London and Manchester.

Yet we have our Five Points, our emigrant quarters, our swarms of seamstresses to whom their utmost toil in monotonous daily drudgery gives only bare subsistence, a life barren of hope and of enjoyment; our hordes of dock thieves, and of children who live in the streets and by them. No one can walk the length of Broadway without meeting some hideous troop of ragged girls, from twelve years old down, brutalized already almost beyond redemption by premature vice, clad in the filthy refuse of the rag-picker's collections, obscene of speech, the stamp of childhood gone from their faces, hurrying along with harsh laughter and foulness on their lips that some of them have learned by rote, yet too young to understand it; with thief written in their cunning eyes and whore on their depraved faces, though so unnatural, foul, and repulsive in every look and gesture, that that last profession seems utterly beyond their aspirations. On a rainy day such crews may be seen by dozens. They haunt every other crossing and skulk away together, when the sun comes out and the mud is dry again. And such a group I think the most revolting object that the social diseases of a great city can produce. A gang of blackguard boys is lovely by the side of it.

Meantime, philanthropists are scolding about the fugitive slave law, or shedding tears over the wretched niggers of the Carolinas who have to work and eat their victuals on principles inconsistent with the rights of man, or agitating because the unhanged scoundrels in the City Prison occupy cells imperfectly ventilated. "Scholars" are laboriously writing dissertations for the Historical Society on the First Settlement of the Township of Squankum, and consuming the midnight oil in elucidating and illustrating the highly interesting MS collection of letters in the possession of the Smith family supposed to have been written by Petrus Smith who died somewhere about 1690, to the great weariness and dreariness of the patient men who attend the meetings of that association. Clergymen are compiling treatises on Ancient Egypt, or evolving windiness that they imbibed "under the shadow of Mont Blanc."

And what am I doing, I wonder? I'm neither scholar nor philanthropist nor clergyman, nor in any capacity a guide or ruler of the people, to be sure—there is that shadow of an apology for my sitting still. But if Heaven will permit and enable me, I'll do something in the matter before I die—to have helped one dirty vagabond child out of such a pestilential sink would be a thing one would not regret when one came to march out of this world—and if one looks at FACTS, would be rather more of an achievement than the writing another *Iliad.*

OCTOBER 20, MONDAY

Half-past twelve P.M. Thank God, we are happily at the end of today—the first great peril is over. Ellie was very bright through the morning; played a game of chequers with me, read aloud, and so forth, her pains occurring every ten minutes or thereabouts. She dined here in the library, and by six o'clock the pains were much more frequent and began to be severe. At about 7:30, she went to bed in a good deal of suffering, and from that time till the finale, suffered terribly, though I suppose no more than is the common lot of women. She bore up bravely, only begging sometimes for chloroform, which Johnston most stoically and imperturbably declined giving. My nerves tingle yet at the remembrance of her cries and struggles of pain. But at ten minutes after ten her baby was born, a boy, and they say a very fine one; certainly vociferous—his ululations first informed me that he had come into the world.

1852

Daniel Webster died, lamented by fewer than would have been the case had he not been the proponent of the Compromise of 1850. John Jay, a grandson of the first chief justice, was one of those who could never forgive this alleged betrayal of the antislavery cause.

Strong shared the wide public interest in spiritualism. Margaret and Kate Fox, daughters of a farmer in Wayne County, New York, had made a sensation in Rochester where their table rappings were interpreted as the work of spirits, and in 1850 they had come to New York to hold highly profitable seances much publicized by Horace Greeley in the *Tribune*. "Spirit circles" had sprung up, and the city witnessed the advent of scores of new media. There were even periodicals on the subject, the most popular being *The Spiritual Telegraph*.

William Makepeace Thackeray made the first of his American lecture tours in this year. His subject was English humorists of the eighteenth century. The "Mr. Astor" who left his card on the novelist was William B. Astor, son of John Jacob Astor and probably the richest man in America.

MAY 15, SATURDAY

Thursday evening, Charles and Eleanor and James Lydig and Lydig Suydam, Walter Cutting and Ellie and I went off to 78 Twenty-sixth Street and had a private interview with Mrs. Fish and her knocking spirits, and then came back here and had some supper. The knockers are much talked of now, from Edmonds' extraordinary publications in the *Shekinah*. One of his two articles is a mere rhapsody or parable, very obscure and ill-written, but the other is meant to be a statement of facts, a vision of Heaven and Hell in which Benjamin Franklin and William Penn and Sir Isaac Newton and the late Mrs. Edmonds appear and express their views. Sir Isaac informs the Judge that he made a great mistake about the Law of Gravitation and the Judge adds a note stating that he had been convinced that it was so for a great many years.

I suppose the vision is a tolerably faithful record of a vivid waking dream produced by opium, drink, and mental excitement. The developments of this spiritual school have become very extraordinary and extensive. Besides their quarterly periodical printed at Bridgeport, they have one or two newspapers in this city, and I believe others published elsewhere. There is a stout little duodecimo volume consisting of "communications" from George Washington, Jefferson, Andrew Jackson, Margaret Fuller, and a great many other people, all of them writing very remarkably alike, and most of them very questionable grammar. People publish statements of extraordinary visitations made them by six individuals "in ancient costume," who promenade about for a long while and finally disappear, leaving Hebrew and Sanscrit MSS behind them, not specially relevant to anything. Edgar A. Poe spells out bad imitations of the poetry he wrote while in the flesh. Tables loaded with heavy weights are made to dance vigorously. . . . It is a strange chapter in the history of human credulity at all events, and as such worth investigating.

OCTOBER 25

Webster died early yesterday morning, and seems from the brief notices that have come here by telegraph to have made a stately exit, to have died self-possessed, thoughtful, and resigned, in style fitting his great career and his lofty place in the eyes of Europe and America. It is the ending of one of the greatest men of this time; one of the greatest intellectually, not morally. His position in the North would have been far more commanding if there had been moral weight in his character. But love of office and improvidence in his private affairs sometimes made him do things unheroic to gain place or money. There was undue love of brandy and water, too.

Still, everyone felt confidence in his ability to do all he undertook. All complications foreign or domestic were felt to be in a fair way towards settlement when Daniel had once laid hands on them. Everybody of all parties, except a few phrenetic abolitionists and ismatizens like John Jay, feels this, and the sense of loss is more general and deeper than in any like case I have known. Horace Greeley is resigned and submissive, to be sure.

Jay was "on the point of leaving church" yesterday, being greatly outraged and lacerated by some remarks in poor little Bedell's sermon about the calamity the country had sustained.

Music sheet cover for *Funeral March to the Memory of . . . Daniel Webster*, lithograph by J. H. Bufford, c. 1852. (National Portrait Gallery)

November 21, Sunday Afternoon

At Thackeray's first lecture Friday night, with Ellie. Subject, Swift. Lecture very effective, clear, and truthful. Specially pleased with the plain-spoken, masculine tone of its criticism on Swift and his books. He handled him without regard to conventionalities, spoke of the man as he deserved, were he ten times as great in intellect. Freedom from humbug is the central point of Thackeray's constitution. . . .

November 28

This has been quite a dissipated week in a small way. Monday night, Thackeray's lecture on Congreve and Addison. Very judicious view of the drama of the reign of Charles II; the sterling old English drama discussed with plainness of speech. Tuesday, Miss Margaret Lydig dined here and George Anthon. . . .

My respect for Thackeray increases with each successive lecture. It's not merely their manner that's attractive—their substance is sound and true, and often original.

December 4

Two more lectures by Thackeray, spirited and original, though not so striking as the first two. They are still crowded. . . .

Lamentable commentary on the Vanity of Human Greatness in Thackeray's inquiry of Bancroft, "Who is a Mr. Astor who has left a card for me?"

December 9, Thursday

Thackeray's final lecture Monday night was one of his very best. I came near a disagreeable scrape. The crowd and heat were such that Ellie came pretty near fainting, and only saved herself by concentrated exertion of *will*. If she *had* succumbed, getting her out through the close-packed aisle and into a carriage would have been no comfortable task. . . .

1853–1855

Louis Napoleon Bonaparte became emperor of the French as Napoleon III, much to the disgust of Strong who remembered him as a penniless and dissolute pretender in the bars of New York.

Strong's contemptuous reference to "Bloomers" (radical feminists) on September 8, 1853, shows his extreme conservatism in matters of the emancipation of women. The name was derived from that of Amelia Bloomer, editor of the feminist newspaper *Lily*, and it applied to a "costume" introduced by Elizabeth Smith Miller as a "symbol of the suffrage movement." Strong's attitude was never to change, and we shall see him even disapproving the admission of women to the bar.

The new governor of New York in 1853, Horatio Seymour, a Democrat, vigorously opposed the extremist factions of prohibition and abolition. Despite the interest aroused in favor of the former by the meeting of the World's Temperance Convention in Metropolitan Hall, he vetoed a bill of the legislature, modeled on one recently passed in Maine, that would have outlawed the sale of alcoholic beverages. Strong was opposed to the radical abolitionists, but was inclined to favor some degree of prohibition.

These years mark the intensification of Strong's lifelong interest in music. The music historian, Vera Brodsky Lawrence, is preparing a three-volume work, *Strong on Music*, to study and evaluate his comments on concerts, operas, and other musical attractions contained in the diary.

The entry on October 24, 1854, refers to James Foster, Jr., a rich merchant on whose generosity many citizens had vainly counted to endow an opera house in New York.

OPPOSITE: *The Bloomer Costume*, lithograph by Nathaniel Currier, 1851. Strong writes of a "great shindy between Bloomers and anti-Bloomers" at the Temperance Convention. (MCNY)

1853

I maintain the cause of the French Empress sturdily in these times, with no very tangible reason except that she has auburn hair and Eugénie is a very pretty name. I rather like the notion of Napoleon III, who, ten or twelve years ago, was a disreputable, dirty, drinking, penniless, foreign prince prowling about these streets and ordered out of the bar room of the old Washington Hall (where Stewart's shop is now) because he was too great a loafer to be allowed to hang about even those disreputable premises, who had so long been wriggling in the gutters and Cloaca of the social system, being now on terms of equality with kings and czars, and making something his friends call a *mésalliance* with the beautiful representative of one of the first among the haughtiest nobility in Europe. There's a romance about it that's altogether refreshing. It will be a curious chapter for readers of history in 1953. As to the attacks on the young Empress's fair fame, I utterly renounce them. *Vivat* Donna Eugenia. . . .

SEPTEMBER 8, THURSDAY

Steamer *Bay State* in trouble last night; something or other connected with her crank or her walking-beam knocked in the head of her cylinder, and that long saloon was filled with scalding steam. Great shindy between Bloomers and anti-Bloomers, at the Temperance Convention in session here. As for the "Rev." Antoinette Brown & Co., I should be glad to see them respectfully pumped upon by a crowd of self-appointed conservators of manners and morals, though perhaps they have womanhood enough left in spite of themselves to be worthy of better usage. The strumpets of Leonard and Church streets are not *much* further below the ideal of womanhood than these loathsome dealers in clack, who seek to change women into garrulous men without virility. I'm glad I'm too stolid tonight for full realization of their folly. It would lead surely to a sick headache tomorrow. Womanhood is still reverenced in this irreverent age and country, as every omnibus and railroad car can testify. Destroy its claim to concession and protection and courtesy by putting it on an equality in everything but physical strength with manhood, and manhood is gone, too. . . .

1854

APRIL 1

Governor Seymour has vetoed the Maine Liquor Law. Whether he's right or wrong is a question on which an off-hand opinion is clearly presumptuous, for the questions involved are deep and dubious. I've no sort of sympathy with the temperance fanatics—rather a prejudice against them. But I am sure it would be better for mankind if alcohol were extinguished and annihilated. Has or has not society the right to make it contraband, as it forbids the sale or storage of gunpowder within certain limits, as it . . . assumes a right to confiscate and destroy a beauteous print brought into the custom-house from Paris? I don't know. If the popular voice demands this kind of legislation, we shall have it, and with the support of popular sentiment it will be enforced. Otherwise, the law will probably not be enacted, and if enacted will certainly not be enforced. The democratic despotism of a majority is a formidable element of injustice and oppression, but it is the power to which we are subject and which will determine this question.

Son of Temperance, **lithograph by Nathaniel Currier, 1848. The Pledge: "No Brother shall make, buy, sell, or use as a beverage, any spirituous or malt, liquors, wine or cider." (MCNY)**

OVERLEAF: *The Drunkard's Progress*, **lithograph by Nathaniel Currier, 1846. Although Strong admits no sympathy with "temperance fanatics," he is "sure it would be better for mankind if alcohol were extinguished and annihilated." (MCNY)**

STEP 1.
A glass
with
a Friend.

STEP 2.
A glass to
keep the
cold out.

STEP 3.
A glass
too
much.

STEP 4.
Drunk
and
riotous.

JUNE 20

After the everlasting rains of the spring, we are entering on a period of drowth. The sun sets, a well-defined, coppery disk like a red-hot penny in a dark room, and all the western sky is curtained with dull, coppery haze. Cholera is in town, and pretty active—fifty-odd deaths last week. But many of these cases were doubtless aggravated diarrhœa and cholera morbus, and all are thus far confined to the lowest and filthiest classes, whose existence from one day to another in their atmosphere of morphic influences is a triumph of vital organization and illustrates the vigorous tenacity of life (under the deadliest conditions) bestowed on the human species. But we may well be destined to undergo an epidemic this summer. Coleridge's Cologne was not more fetid or mephitic than this metropolis. The stinks of Centre Street lift up their voices. Malarious aromata rampage invisible through every street, and in the second-rate regions of the city, such as Cherry Street, poor old Greenwich Street, and so on, atmospheric poison and pungent foetor and gaseous filth cry aloud and spare not, and the wayfaring man inhales at every breath a pair of lungs full of vaporized decomposing gutter mud and rottenness. Alas for our civic rulers, whose office it is to see that this be not so. . . .

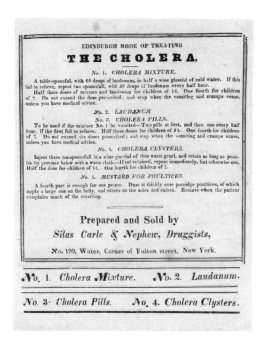

Advertisement for cholera cures. (MCNY)

OCTOBER 11

Today will long be had in bitter remembrance by many. Those to whom its sad news announced no personal calamity and private grief will not soon forget the general mournful excitement and agitation that stopped all the workings of Wall Street this morning and kept brokers and lawyers and business men of all sorts around the newspaper offices and telegraphs all day long.

There was no serious feeling of uneasiness about the *Arctic* yesterday. It was taken for granted that she had put back in consequence of the breaking of a shaft or some such accident. I was at the Novelty Works yesterday afternoon (with Henry Youngs, about furnaces for Trinity Chapel) and talked of the missing steamer with Horatio Allen. He "wasn't anxious," there couldn't have been anything serious the matter, unless possibly fire, and that was not very likely. There would be news this morning by the Cunard steamer. I was waked this morning by the voices of the newsboys, something about "the *Arctic* and four hundred lives," and sent out at once for the extra.

What a chill that proclamation must have sent into scores of households! How many people sprang up at the sound of that half-inarticulate nasal cry, and hurried off to get the paper and refused to entertain the idea that they had heard the announcement aright, and paid their sixpences and unfolded their purchase in desperate haste, and saw the terrible truth in print! Allen, I. G. Pearson, Joseph Brown, Woodruff—to those households and many more it was the voice of death.

On Wednesday, the 27th September, the *Arctic*, being about 40 miles off Cape Race, in a dense fog, going at full speed, ran into, or was run into, by an iron-propeller steamer. What became of the propeller nobody pretends to say. It is generally supposed that she foundered with all on board. The *Arctic* floated for a time, probably about four hours, and then sank. Many of her crew are saved. Nearly all her two hundred passengers perished.

Three of E. K. Collins's family, wife, son, and daughter, my old tutor Abner Benedict and his wife, Woodruff (W. & Leonard) Lord's brother-in-law, Asaph Stone and his wife and young daughter, poor little George Pearson, young William Brown and his wife (daughter of Charles Moulton) and their child, his sister, George F. Allen, wife and child (Mrs. Allen another sister of Brown's), Edward Sandford, LeRoy Newbold, Captain Luce, Babcock in Twenty-second Street, George S. Howland the Brooklyn operator, and many others of whom I had more or less knowledge are lost. There is a faint possibility that some may have been saved in the boats, or picked up. Gilbert (G., Cobb,

OVERLEAF: *Wreck of the U.S.M. Steamship Arctic, Off Cape Race, Wednesday, September 27, 1854,* lithograph by Currier & Ives, 1854. (MCNY)

& Johnson), who was thought to have perished, has reached Halifax, with a nephew of Gibson's and two or three other passengers and a large detachment of the crew.

Captain Luce stuck to the ship with his only child, a boy of fourteen and a cripple. He refused to entrust the child to Bahlaam, the second officer. I understand from Gourlie (who had it from Dorian, the third officer) that Luce had no confidence in Bahlaam, and that Bahlaam showed sufficient reason for that want of confidence by leaving the ship with the boat in which he'd been ordered to keep astern or alongside and help construct the raft.

It is a sickening business; worse, I think, than the *Lexington* tragedy of fourteen years ago, worse even than the butchery on board the *Henry Clay,* at least in the number lost. There is a very unpleasant disproportion between the number of the crew and of the passengers known to have been saved. To be sure, self-preservation is the common instinct of waiter and fireman, Wall Street broker and Fifth Avenue millionaire, and the strong-armed sailors and engineers can't be blamed perhaps for acting on their earlier information of the extent of the peril and using their superior strength to fill the boats and save themselves. But it's hard to think of the scores of delicate women whose only chance of safety was thus destroyed, and who were left to perish without hope. It was the business of the officers to keep all hands under control and to provide what little help there was first for those who were least able to help themselves.

OCTOBER 24

A messenger from Wall Street with the news that James Foster (*Count* Foster, the leader of forlorn hopes for the endowment of opera) was very ill and wanted to see me. Went forthwith to his house in Bond Street. The servant said he was very sick indeed, with the "diaree," and no better. Waited awhile in his gorgeously decorated drawing room, and was then shewn upstairs. Found him in bed; Francis and Clinton (relation of his first wife) in attendance. Very clear-headed and collected. Had been attacked with usual forewarning of cholera Saturday, had neglected it, had gone to E. K. Collin's place in Westchester Sunday, had been rather sick yesterday, and early this morning found his disorder taking a very formidable shape. . . .

Came home, drafted and copied the will, and was at Foster's again by a little after five. Waited an hour and a half before going upstairs. The news received from time to time shewed that he had been and was losing ground. And as I sat in the splendidly furnished suite of rooms, with the gilded and frescoed ceilings and paneled walls to which he'd given so much care, I heard now and then the groans from where their proprietor was agonizing with cramp. Went to him at last, and saw at once that his case was very bad and unpromising. Found the doctors (to whom was added Kissam, I think) had given him up; his hand was cold, face darkened, skin of the fingers corrugated, articulation thick. I read over the will very warily and distinctly, pausing at each material clause for a sign of assent, which I received. He said it was all right, but he wanted a codicil, about a $5,000 legacy. Sat down in the sick room to draw it, with the doctors, the wife, the weeping daughter, and all sorts of tragic elements all around me. Foster beckoned to Carter and told him that I'd omitted the affix of *Junior* to his name. Had to see his wife hanging over him, and to hear him say, "Well, Julia, this is the last night we shall be together"; had to watch his cool, deliberate effort to sign, with fingers stiffened by cramp; had to wait for a minute or two, I suppose, though it seemed like half an hour, while Francis was rubbing the hand, and while the patient's blue, thin lips were retracted on his set teeth, till he could laboriously construct his signature. . . .

NOVEMBER 8

We are so young a people that we feel the want of nationality, and delight in whatever asserts our national "American" existence. We have not, like England and France, centuries of achievement and calamities to look back on; we have no *record* of Americanism and we feel its want. Hence the development, in every state of the Union, of "Historical Societies" that seize on and seal up every worthless reminiscence of our colonial and revolutionary times. We crave a history, instinctively, and being without the eras that belong to older nationalities—Anglo-Saxon, Carolingian, Hohenstauffen, Ghibelline, and so forth—we dwell on the details of our little all of historic life, and venerate every trivial fact about our first settlers and colonial governors and revolutionary heroes. A vivid narrative of the life and manners of New York fifty years ago would be received with enthusiasm here. London would take comparatively little interest in such a picture of the times of Pitt and Fox.

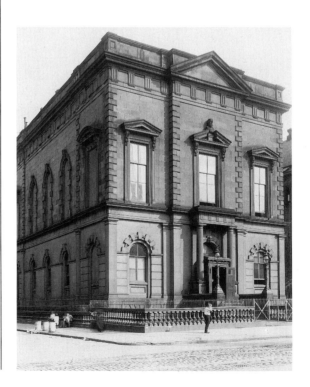

In 1857, The New York Historical Society, founded in 1804, moved into its seventh home, at the corner of Second Avenue and 11th Street. Philip Hone had been a vice president of the Society. (NYHS)

JANUARY 21

The unemployed workmen, chiefly Germans, are assembling daily in the Park and listening to inflammatory speeches by demagogues who should be "clapt up" for preaching sedition and marching in procession through the streets. The large majority of the distressed multitude is decently clad and looks well fed and comfortable. People anticipate riot and disturbance; there have been two or three rumors of it in various quarters. Friday night it was rumored that a Socialist mob was sacking the Schiff mansion in the Fifth Avenue, where was a great ball and mass meeting of the aristocracy. Certainly the destitute are a thankless set and deserve little sympathy in their complaints. The efforts to provide employment and relief, the activity of individuals and of benevolent organizations, the readiness with which money is contributed do credit to the city. More could be done and ought to be done, of course, but what is done is beyond precedent here, and more than our "unemployed" friends had a right to count on.

There has been vast improvement during the last three or four years in the dealings of our "upper class" with the poor; not merely in the comparative abundance of their bounty, but in the fact that it has become fashionable and creditable and not unusual for people to busy themselves in personal labors for the very poor and in personal intercourse with them. It is a very significant thing and would have been held a marvel ten years ago that women like Mrs. Eleanor Curtis, Mrs. Lewis Jones, Miss Field, Mrs. Peters, Miss Gibbs, and others should be working hard in "ragged schools" and the like. Perhaps it may be but a short-lived fashion, but it is an indication most encouraging of progress toward social health. . . .

Thursday night at Mrs. Robert Gracie's third and (happily) last *reception.* Such transactions are sheer lunacy. The house is small, and the rooms were hot and crowded, so that one moved about like a fly in a glue pot through a stifling, viscid, glutinous medium of perspiring humanity and dilute carbonic acid gas. In the plenitude of their folly, people actually cleared away a narrow space in the middle room, where half a dozen idiotic couples polkaed and waltzed to a faintly audible piano-jingle, increasing thereby the pressure on the house to one hundred atmospheres. The crowd must have nearly burst out the walls. . . .

JANUARY 27

Walter Scott, in 1803 or 1804, surely felt and knew the lives and manners and rights and wrongs of Englishmen and Scotsmen then living and daily meeting him and dining with him even better and more deeply than the ways of his beloved Border moss-troopers and feudal barons. Why should he not have brought his great genius to bear on *them* rather than on institutions and ways of thinking that had perished three hundred years before? . . . The poet of A.D. 1855 will have his hands full with the men and women and things of 1855, and has no right to go back to other dead times, "revolutionary," mediaeval, classical, or patriarchal. His hand and his heart find enough to feel and to do at his own door. There is poetry enough latent in the South Street merchant and the Wall Street financier; in Stewart's snobby clerk chaffering over ribbons and laces; in the omnibus driver that conveys them all from the day's work to the night's relaxation and repose; in the brutified denizen of the Points and the Hook; in the sumptuous star courtesan of Mercer Street thinking sadly of her village home; in the Fifth Avenue ballroom; in the Grace Church contrast of eternal vanity and new bonnets; in the dancers at Lewis Jones's and Mr. Schiff's, and in the future of each and all.

MARCH 25

Wagner's Overture to *Tannhäuser* also played, a composition on which I'd rather not commit myself till after a rehearing. Novel, most elaborate, and full of *talent,* clearly, but not altogether pleasing, and whether truly original and genial or merely outré and labored I can't say. . . .

ARIL 17, TUESDAY

Trinity Chapel duly consecrated this morning. I didn't get into Wall Street till three o'clock. The services were well conducted and impressive; church packed full, of course. I was there at nine and found people assembling. Fussed about with Livingston and others for an hour and three-quarters between the chapel and the two houses opposite, where the clergy and others assembled—making arrangements and keenly sensible of my own importance. The entering procession was imposing; sextons of the church and chapels with very big staves gilded and colored in the early decorated style; the "parochial" churchwardens with lesser staves (like the pointers used by lecturers to indicate and demonstrate on their diagrams), which the committee had licensed them to "bear" on their solemn written request. I wanted to give them letters-patent authorizing cocked hats, also. Lots of clergy in surplices. Happily, it was a fine day and the distance walked by the procession very small, so they did not have to wear their hats and present the appearance of a holiday turnout of cartmen in clean frocks. The university cap or some ecclesiastical headpiece is wanted on such occasions. The string of fifty or sixty priests and deacons, and as many divinity students, passed into the chapel under my nose as "we" received them on the chapel porch, and I must say I was not favorably impressed by my review of their physiognomies. They don't contrast so very advantageously with the Roman Catholic clergy against whose outward appearance so much is said, except in point of cleanliness. If one must judge of their physiognomy, they are below the average trader, physician, attorney even, in expression, moral and intellectual. There were sensual pig-faces, white vacant sheep-faces, silly green gosling-faces, solemn donkey-faces; but the prevailing type was that of the commonplace fourth-rate snob, without any particular expression but mediocrity and grim professional Pharisaism. Here and there was a nice, manly, earnest face, now and then, among the elder clergy, one that shewed energy and cleanness. But they were mostly a sad set. Why does that profession attract so few men of mark, moral vigor, and commanding talent?

1856

This and the next three years find Strong increasingly apprehensive that civil strife may not be avoided. His attitude toward the Southern planters was hardening, but he still maintained that slavery was not a wrong *per se*. His concern was the preservation of the Union at almost any price.

The widening gulf between North and South was reflected in the bitter struggle in Congress over the speakership of the House, which resulted in the election of a Republican, regarded as a triumph by abolitionists and one that might herald the defeat of the unpopular Democratic administration of President Franklin Pierce.

JANUARY 8, TUESDAY

This is a stern winter. Saturday's snowstorm was the severest for many years past. The street are like Jordan, "hard roads to travel." One has to walk warily over the slippery sidewalks and to plunge madly over crossings ankle-deep in snow, in order to get uptown and down, for the city railroads are still impracticable and walking (with all its discomforts) is not so bad as the great crowded sleigh-caravans that have taken the place of the omnibi. These insane vehicles carry each its hundred sufferers, whom about half have to stand in the wet straw with their feet freezing and occasionally stamped on by their fellow travelers, their ears and noses tingling in the bitter wind, their hats always on the point of being blown off. When the chariot stops, they tumble forward, and when it starts again, they tumble backward, and when they arrive at the end of their ride, they commonly land up to their knees in a snowdrift, through which they flounder as best they may, to escape the little fast-trotting vehicles that are coming straight at them. Many of the cross streets are still untraveled by anything on wheels or runners, but in Broadway, the Bowery, and other great thoroughfares, there is an orgasm of locomotion. It's more than a carnival; it's a wintry dionysiaca.

MAY 29, THURSDAY

No new vagaries from the wild men of the South since yesterday. The South is to the North nearly what the savage Gaelic race of the Highlands was to London *tempore* William and Mary, *vide* Macaulay's third volume; except that they've assumed to rule their civilized neighbors instead of being oppressed by them, and that the simple, barbaric virtues of their low social development have been thereby deteriorated.

A few fine specimens have given them a prestige the class don't deserve. We at the North are a busy money-making democracy, comparatively law-abiding and peace-loving, with the faults (among others) appropriate to traders and workers. A rich Southern aristocrat who happens to be of fine nature, with the self-reliance and high tone that life among an aristocracy favors, and culture and polish from books and travel, strikes us (not as Brooks struck Sumner but) as something different from ourselves, more ornamental and in some respects better. He has the polish of a highly civilized society, with the qualities that belong to a ruler of serfs. Thus a notion has got footing here that "Southern gentlemen" are a high-bred chivalric aristocracy, something like Louis XIV's noblesse, with grave faults, to be sure, but on the whole, very gallant and generous, regulating themselves by "codes of honor" (that are *wrong,* of course, but very grand); not rich, but surrounded by all the elements of real refinement. Whereas I believe they are, in fact, a race of lazy, ignorant, coarse, sensual, swaggering, sordid, beggarly barbarians, bullying white men and breeding little niggers for sale. The exceptions prove no more that's in favor of the class than Lochiel or "Fergus McIvor" can prove in favor of Highland civilization. Or a parallel might be drawn between the South Carolina statesman and fire-eater, and the Irish politician descended from Brian Boru, proud of his own beautiful Ireland, oppressed by Saxons, ready to give satisfaction to any political opponent, full of gas and brag and bosh. But it would be unfair to the Celtic gentleman.

OVERLEAF: *Sleighing in New York,* lithograph by Thomas Benecke, 1855. In writing about the severity of a winter storm, Strong states that many "cross streets are still untraveled by anything on wheels or runners, but in Broadway, the Bowery, and other great thoroughfares, there is an orgasm of locomotion. It's more than a carnival; it's a wintry dionysiaca." (NYHS)

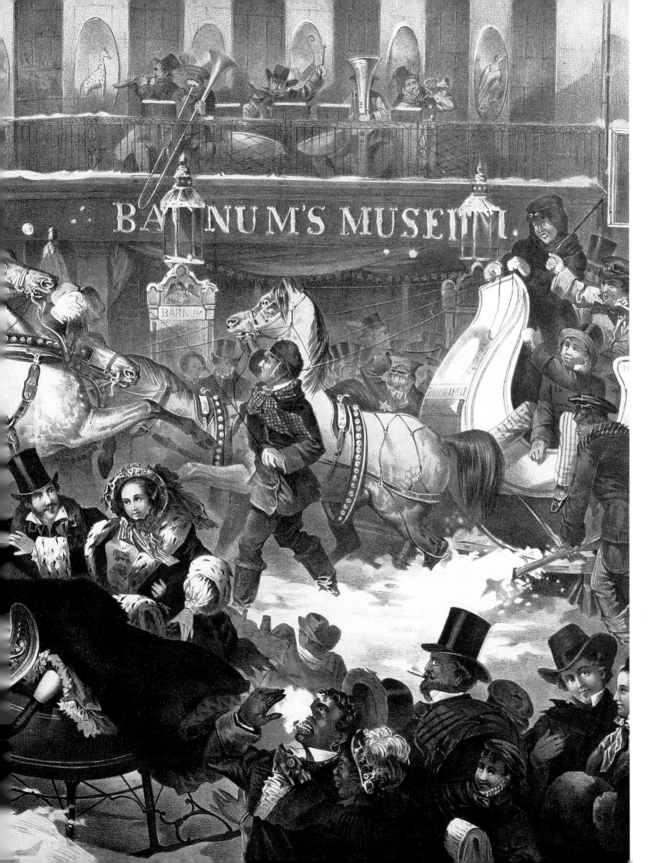

August 5

Long talk with Charles Kuhn this afternoon over the affairs of the nation. My platform is substantially this:

1. Slavery is not a wrong per se. If it were so, the states in which it exists ought to right it. We are not called on to interfere with it, supposing it a wrong, any more than we are bound to attack the serfdom of Russia or the iniquities of Naples. And there are so many practical difficulties in the way of righting it that the people who are in that case bound to act, the South, may be pardoned for pausing and hesitating and acting reluctantly. . . .

2. The practical working of the institution (whether it be in itself a wrong or not) includes iniquities that are probably curable by legislation, but are, perhaps, of its essence—inseparable: the selling asunder of families, remediless cruelty and oppression, enforced concubinage, incest, and so forth.

3. It practically demoralizes and degrades the whole community where it exists.

4. It operates against the material development and the progress in civilization and wealth of such community, and is guilty of the difference between Virginia and New York.

5. Any interference by Northern states or individuals with the legal institutions of the Southern states, which is calculated to produce disaffection or disorder in their servile class, being not merely gratuitous, but most perilous to the insecure social system of those unhappy communities, ought to be repressed most sternly. The North would be merely acting in good faith if it made such interference a capital crime.

6. Congress has no power over any feature of the institution as it exists in a Southern state.

7. But it has power to legislate for the territories, and it may and should exclude from those territories while under its jurisdiction an institution which has thus far only done harm wherever it exists. When those territories have been set up in business for themselves, they may legislate as they please, and introduce slavery into their system if they are fools enough to do it.

Pity I'm not in the Senate of the United States!

OCTOBER 29

It strikes me that this institution—slavery as it *exists* at the South with all its "safe-guards" and "necessary legislation"—is the greatest crime on the largest scale known in modern history; taking into account the time it has occupied, the territory it covers, the number of its subjects, and the civilization of the criminals. It is deliberate legislation intended to extinguish and annihilate the moral being of men for profit; systematic murder, not of the physical, but of the moral and intellectual being; blasphemy, not in word, but in systematic action against the Spirit of God which dwells in the souls of men to elevate, purify, and ennoble them. So I feel now; perhaps it's partly the dominant election furor that colors my notions. Of course, slaveholders are infinitely better than their system. And we have nothing to say about this system where it is established, and we have no right to interfere with it, no responsibility for it. The question for the North is whether we shall help establish it elsewhere, in the "territories" our nation owns.

DECEMBER 11

Went to *La Traviata.* . . . *Traviata* is utter drivel. I could write as bad an opera myself. To call it bad is to do it more than justice; it has not strength enough to stand alone or to *be* anything. It is definable by the negation of every good quality.

DECEMBER 18

Very great big party at William B. Astor's Monday night, and another last night at John C. Hamilton's. Both were favorable specimens of their bad class, particularly the former.

1857

A financial panic that began in New York and rapidly spread across the nation produced poverty and riots.

Frederick Law Olmstead (who during the Civil War would be a co-member with Strong of the Sanitary Commission) and Calvert Vaux submitted their plans for the proposed new Central Park and were commissioned its architects. This scrubby tract of rocky land, dotted with a few farms and shanties, forming a huge rectangle in the middle of Manhattan, had been purchased by the city in 1856. Work began in 1857, and by the mid-sixties one enthusiast exclaimed: "On a bare, unsightly and disgusting spot, they (the Park Commissioners) have created an area of beauty, charming as the Garden of the Lord."

Lawlessness had increased with the exploding population of the city and massive immigration from Europe. Organized gangs—the Dead Rabbits, the Empire Club, the Five Pointers, and Mike Walsh's Spartan Band—fought in the streets, almost unimpeded by a corrupt constabulary. In response to public outrage, the state legislature created a new Metropolitan police force, but a shameless mayor, Fernando Wood, refused to instate it, and the intervention of Federal troops was required to enforce the new law. A riot growing out of a brawl between the Dead Rabbits and the Five Pointers, before the difference between the old and new police forces had been settled, reduced the city to near chaos. It was quelled at last by the Seventh Regiment.

OPPOSITE: *Wall Street, Half Past Two, Oct. 13, 1857,* painting by James H. Cafferty and Charles G. Rosenberg. A dramatic moment in the Panic of 1857, the county's worst depression in twenty years. In the background is the present Trinity Church, designed by Richard Upjohn and finished in 1846. (MCNY)

FEBRUARY 1

An epidemic of crime this winter. "Garroting" stories abound, some true, some no doubt fictitious, devised to explain the absence of one's watch and pocketbook after a secret visit to some disreputable place, or to put a good face on some tipsy street fracas. But a tradesman was attacked the other afternoon in broad daylight at his own shop door in the Third Avenue near Thirteenth Street by a couple of men, one of whom was caught, and will probably get his deserts in the State Prison, for life—the doom of two of the fraternity already tried and sentenced. Most of my friends are investing in revolvers and carry them about at night, and if I expected to have to do a great deal of late street-walking off Broadway, I think I should make the like provision; though it's a very bad practice carrying concealed weapons. Moreover, there was an uncommonly shocking murder in Bond Street (No. 31) Friday night; one Burdell, a dentist, strangled and riddled with stabs in his own room by some person unknown who must have been concealed in the room. Motive unknown, evidently not plunder.

FEBRUARY 4

The chief subject of discourse, excluding all others nearly, is the Burdell murder . . . and the extravaganzas and indecencies of that ignorant blackguard the Coroner, Connery, who is conducting from day to day a broad farce called an inquest as afterpiece to the tragedy. . . . I had quite forgotten Burdell. He was frequently in the office a year or fifteen months ago, and used to pay my father interest on a mortgage held by the Lloyd estate. . . .

JULY 4

The customary din is raging without. The Chinese War has raised the price and diminished the supply of firecrackers, but our peace is not thereby promoted. The ingenious youth of the city adopt noisy pistols in their place. . . .

OPPOSITE: Spectators gathered outside 31 Bond Street, scene of the Burdell murder, which Strong says is the "chief subject of discourse, excluding all others nearly," as depicted in *Frank Leslie's Illustrated Newspaper*. (Charles Lockwood)

JULY 5

There was a riot yesterday afternoon in the Sixth Ward, and several persons killed. This afternoon and evening it has been renewed. The Seventh and other regiments are out with ball cartridge. Some of the downtown streets are made impassable by cordons of police, others, I am told, by barricades. A crowd is gathered round the hospital gates in Broadway; many cases of gunshot wounds have been passed in. We're in a "state of siege," and if half the stories one hears be true, in something like a state of anarchy. Rumors of hard fighting round Tompkins Square, in the Second Avenue, in Franklin Square, of houses sacked in the Fifth Avenue near Twenty-eighth Street. Probably lies and gross exaggerations. But the Old Police being disbanded and the New Police as yet inexperienced and imperfectly organized, we are in an insecure and unsettled state at present. I've just returned from prowling cautiously and at a very respectful distance round the seat of war; but I don't know what the disturbance is or has been about. It seems to have been a battle between Irish Blackguardism and Native Bowery Blackguardism, the belligerents afterwards making common cause against the police and uniting to resist their common enemy.

JULY 7

Since Sunday night the city has been peaceable. The "Dead Rabbits" and "Bowery Boys" repose on their respective laurels.

JULY 14

Stroll last night, far down on the east side looking for a mob and finding none. Walked through most of the dangerous regions past Tompkins Square. It appears from the morning papers that I ran some risk of being knocked on the head, of which danger I was wholly ignorant at the time. I saw nothing more alarming than sundry groups of sweaty Teutons jabbering gutturals with vehemence, and smelt no gunpowder, but the explosion of a park of artillery and the magazines would have been required to drown the overpowering, pungent stenches of that region. We're in a very perturbed state again. Riots yesterday and the day before, instigated, some say, by the old police if not by Wood himself. The new police seem very inefficient from want of organization, and a couple of regiments were under arms last night. Should there be occasion for their active intervention, I trust they will fire low and give the blackguardism of the city a sharp lesson. . . . Stroll tonight and lounge round the station house at the corner of Third Street and the Bowery, the outpost or advance guard of law and order. Police scarcely venture east of it. Meetings are being held in the region of Avenue A and near by, with bonfires and gunpowder orations, but I think it is generally known that the militia are under arms and sedition will confine itself to that district, omitting all hostile demonstrations.

JULY 16

Stagnated at home in the evening till half-past ten, when an alarm of fire started me out and I chased the conflagration up Lexington beyond the bounds of civilization into desert places where Irish shanties began to prevail, and the region being lonely and suspicious and the fire still a dozen streets beyond and nearly out beside, I came back perspiring. It was a varnish factory in the latitude of fifty-fifth Street. Coroner's inquest in progress over the unlucky German, Miller or Muller, the "opfer" of the 17th Ward riot. Evidence hopelessly conflicting; impossible to form an opinion whether he was killed by the police or by one of his own party. . . . some say that if the verdict be not against the police, there will be a grand insurrection and a provisional government proclaimed in Tompkins Square.

OVERLEAF: *The Life of a Fireman. The New Era. Steam and Muscle,* lithograph by Currier & Ives, 1861. By this time, the steam pumper had begun to supercede the old hand-powered model, but for several years more both systems would show up at fires. (MCNY)

1858

In 1857 two frigates, one American and one British, were assigned the task of laying an Atlantic cable starting from Ireland. The strand broke. In 1858 a new plan was devised. Two cable-laying vessels met in the middle of the Atlantic, spliced their cable ends, and started laying in opposite directions. Three attempts failed; the fourth was successful. In two months' time the cable broke, but not before President James Buchanan had exchanged greetings with Queen Victoria.

The Crystal Palace, erected in 1852 on a site to the west of the present Public Library in Bryant Park as a display space for arts and sciences, burned to the ground in about fifteen minutes. It had been inspired by the London Crystal Palace of 1851 and was the first large iron and glass structure in America. Although it was reputedly fireproof, wood and other combustible materials used in the interior caught fire, and the whole structure collapsed.

AUGUST 10

Everybody all agog about the Atlantic Cable. Telegraph offices in Wall Street decorated with the flags of all nations and sundry fancy pennons beside, suspended across the street. Newspapers full of the theme, and of the demonstrations the event has produced from New Orleans to Portland. The *Agamemnon* has brought her end safe to Valentia, so the whole cable is now in position. Newspapers vie with each other in gas and grandiloquence. Yesterday's *Herald* said that the cable (or perhaps Cyrus W. Field, uncertain which) is undoubtedly the Angel in the Book of Revelation with one foot on sea and one foot on land, proclaiming that Time shall be no longer. Moderate people merely say that this is the greatest human achievement in history. Possibly not the very greatest; some few things have surely been done in the old time before us that run the cable rather hard. Morse's first forty miles of telegraph wire included this, and much more that shall be hereafter (perhaps), and the first message between Washington and Baltimore was a grander event than this. Laying this wire rope unbroken across the abysses of the Atlantic was no light undertaking, but success, with all the armories of modern science in the service, is not so much to brag of. Is it success after all? No message has yet been transmitted, and we are not told the reason why.

If no great revolution or cataclysm throw mankind off the track they've been traveling for the last half-century, if the earth doesn't blow up or get foul of a comet and be not rebarbarized by Brigham Young or Red Republicanism,

OPPOSITE: *Atlantic Cable Parade, Sept. 1858,* lithograph by Sarony & Knapp, 1858. Sailors from the *Niagara* carry a model of their cable-laying ship along Broadway, and six horses pull a float with a coil of leftover cable. Strong wrote that everybody was "all agog about the Atlantic Cable." (MCNY)

it will be a strange place in 1958, most unlike what it is now. The diverse races of men certainly seem tending toward development into a living organic unit with railroads and steam-packets for a circulating system, telegraph wires for nerves, and the London *Times* and New York *Herald* for a brain.

Progress of the Century, lithograph by Currier & Ives, 1876. New Yorkers were as proud at mid-century of their country's accomplishments as they would be at its centennial, when this print was made. (MCNY)

OCTOBER 5, TUESDAY

Home again. Left Great Barrington at ten-thirty and brought Ellie and her babies and her Abigails and Miss Josephine safe to town by five. It was an auspicious day for railroad travelers; recent rains had laid the dust, and the air was cool. There was an alarm of fire as we emerged from the tunnel at Thirty-first Street, and a majestic column of smoke was marching southeastwardly across the blue sky, and men said the "Crystal Palace" was on fire. So when we reached the Twenty-seventh Street depot, I put the party in charge of James (the waiter, known as Pam from the likeness he bears the portraits of a British statesman), who met us there, and then "fled fast through sun and shade" up Murray Hill in pursuit of the picturesque *magna comitante caterva.* Up every avenue a miscellaneous aggregate of humanity was racing on the same errand. So scampers a wide area of yellow-fallen leaves down the street of Barrington when smitten suddenly by a strong wind from the northwest. Over our heads was rising and wreathing and flowing onward this grand and ominous torrent of vapor, glowing with golden and coppery tints imparted by the setting sun. My run was hard. I panted and perspired before reaching the scene of action. It was the "Crystal Palace." But before I got there, the dome, roof, and walls had gone down. Only a few iron turrets were standing and some fragments of wall that looked like the wreck of a Brobdignagian aviary. The debris was still flaming and blazing furiously. I contemplated the bonfire awhile and then came off, being tired and wanting my dinner.

So bursts a bubble rather noteworthy in the annals of New York. To be more accurate, the bubble burst some years ago, and this catastrophe merely annihilates the apparatus that generated it. Don't know how the fire broke out. The building must have burned up like a pile of shavings. They said in the crowd that many lives had been lost, the swiftness of the fire having cut off egress from the building in a few moments. But I don't believe it. Anyone thus headed off could have kicked his way out through the walls anywhere.

OVERLEAF: *Burning of the New York Crystal Palace,* lithograph by Currier & Ives, 1858. "So bursts a bubble rather noteworthy in the annals of New York," was Strong's comment. (MCNY)

ABOVE: *Central Park, Winter,
The Skating Pond,* lithograph by
Currier & Ives, 1862. (MCNY)

RIGHT: *Central Park in Winter,*
lithograph by Currier & Ives, n.d.
In less than the five years Strong
predicted in 1859, Central Park
was indeed "a feature of the
city." (MCNY)

1859

On October 16 John Brown, the fiery abolitionist whose crusade had led to the massacre of pro-slavery men at Potawatomie, Kansas, in 1856, led a band of twenty-two followers into Virginia and seized the United States Armory at Harper's Ferry. It was his intention to start a slave insurrection. Colonel Robert E. Lee and a company of United States Marines besieged the armory, and Brown was captured and hanged. The fierce agitations aroused in both North and South hastened the coming war.

JUNE 11

Improved the day by leaving Wall Street early and set off with George Anthon and Johnny to explore the Central Park, which will be a feature of the city within five years and a lovely place in A.D. 1900, when its trees will have acquired dignity and appreciable diameters. Perhaps the city itself will perish before then, by growing too big to live under faulty institutions corruptly administered. Reached the park a little before four, just as the red flag was hoisted—the signal for the blasts of the day. They were all around us for some twenty minutes, now booming far off to the north, now quite near, now distant again, like a desultory "affair" between advanced posts of two great armies. We entered the park at Seventy-first Street, on its east side, and made for "The Ramble," a patch just below the upper reservoir. Its footpaths and plantations are finished, more or less, and it is the first section of the ground that has been polished off and made presentable. It promises very well. So does all the lower park, though now in most ragged condition: long lines of incomplete macadamization, "lakes" without water, mounds of compost, piles of blasted stone, acres of what may be greensward hereafter but is now mere brown earth; groves of slender young transplanted maples and locusts, undecided between life and death, with here and there an arboricultural experiment that has failed utterly and is a mere broomstick with ramifications. Celts, caravans of dirt carts, derricks, steam engines, are the elements out of which our future Pleasaunce is rapidly developing. The work seems pushed with vigor and system, and as far as it has gone, looks thorough and substantial. A small army of Hibernians is distributed over the ground. Narrowness is its chief drawback. One sees quite across this *Rus in Urbe* at many points. This will be less felt as the trees grow. The tract seems to have been judiciously laid out. Roads and paths twist about in curves of artistic tortuosity. A broad avenue, exceptionally straight (at the

OVERLEAF: *Central Park, The Lake*, lithograph by Currier & Ives, 1862. (MCNY)

lower end of the park) with a quadruple row of elms, will look Versailles-y by A.D. 1950. On the Fifth Avenue side, the hideous State Arsenal building stares at students of the picturesque, an eyesore that no landscape gardening can alleviate. Let us hope it will soon be destroyed by an accidental fire. From the summit of the rock mount in which "The Ramble" culminates, and from the little wooden framework of an observatory or signal flag tower thereon erected, the upper reservoir (lying on the north) is an agreeable object, notwithstanding the formalism of its straight lines. Johnny was delighted with his walk. . . .

DECEMBER 2

...Old John Brown was hanged this morning; justly, say I, but his name may be a word of power for the next half-century. It was unwise to give fanaticism a martyr. Why could not Virginia have condescended to lock him up for life in a madhouse? Had Edward Oxford been hanged for shooting at Queen Victoria in 1840, his death would have stirred up scores of silly shopboys to regicide (or reginicide), merely from the inscrutable passion for notoriety; for being thought about and talked about—that has much power over man's vanity. . . .

Old Brown's demeanor has undoubtedly made a great impression. Many heroes of the Newgate Calendar have died game, as he did; but his simplicity and consistency, the absence of fuss, parade and bravado, the strength and clearness of his letters, all indicate a depth of conviction that one does not expect in an Abolitionist (who is apt to be a mere talker and sophist), and that tends to dignify and to ennoble in popular repute the very questionable church of which he is protomartyr. Slavery has received no such blow in my time as his strangulation. There must be a revolution in feeling even in the terrified State of Virginia, unless fresh fuel be added to the flame, as it well may be, within the month. The supporters of any institution are apt to be staggered and startled when they find that any one man, wise or foolish, is so convicted of its wrong and injustices as to acquiesce in being hanged by way of protest against it. So did the first Christian martyrs wake up senators and landed gentlemen and patrician ladies, *tempore* Nero and Diocletian, and so on. One's faith in anything is terribly shaken by anybody who is ready to go to the gallows condemning and denouncing it.

OPPOSITE: *John Brown* (after Louis Ransom), lithograph by Currier & Ives, 1863. Brown on the way to his hanging. Strong commented that "One's faith in anything is terribly shaken by anybody who is ready to go to the gallows condemning and denouncing it." (MCNY)

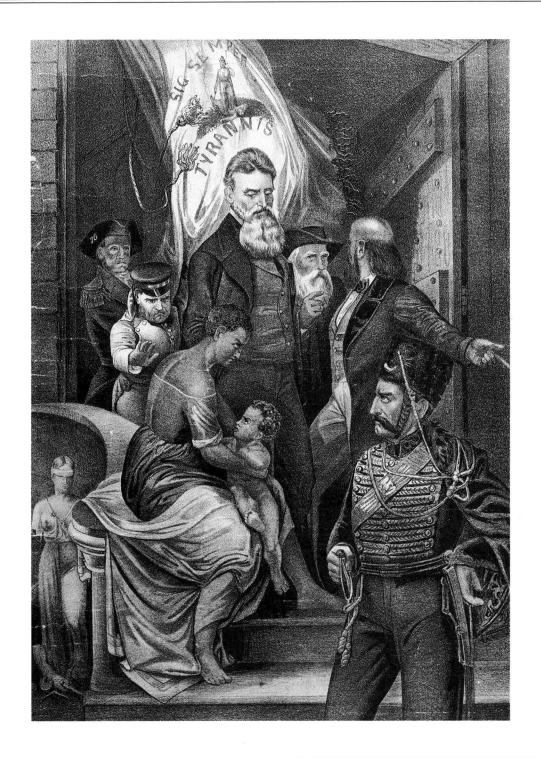

1860

The year that saw the nomination of Abraham Lincoln at the Republican convention was almost dominated in the diary by the state visit to New York of the eighteen-year-old Albert Edward, Prince of Wales, the future King Edward VII.

In Lawrence, Massachusetts, the great Pemberton Mill collapsed, killing some two hundred workers, most of them girls. This tragedy also represented the collapse of utopian experiments in factory labor practices launched in the textile mills of Massachusetts in the 1820s. The workers were exclusively women and children, but they were provided with daily meals, dormitories, and evening entertainment of a moral and educational character. By this time, the flood of immigrants provided even cheaper employees, for whom the niceties could be dispensed with.

P. T. Barnum exhibited a freak advertised as a "What-is-it," which was thought to be a cross between a Negro and some species of large ape. Strong makes a reference to Darwin, whose *Origin of Species* had been published only the year before.

The Democratic convention met in Charleston in April but could not agree on a candidate. Alabama led the defecting seven "cotton states" to a separate convention in Richmond where they nominated John Cabell Breckinridge. The balance of the Democratic delegates adjourned to Baltimore where they nominated Stephen A. Douglas. The split in the party paved the way for the Republican victory in November. Lincoln's election was not acceptable to the South, and South Carolina seceded from the Union on December 20.

JANUARY 11

News today of a fearful tragedy at Lawrence, Massachusetts, one of the wholesale murders commonly known in newspaper literature as accident or catastrophe. A huge factory, long notoriously insecure and ill-built, requiring to be patched and bandaged up with iron plates and braces to stand the introduction of its machinery, suddenly collapsed into a heap of ruins yesterday afternoon without the smallest provocation. Some five or six hundred operatives went down with it—young girls and women mostly. An hour or two later, while people were working frantically to dig out some two hundred still under the ruins, many of them alive and calling for help, some quite unhurt, fire caught in the great pile of debris, and these prisoners were roasted. It is too atrocious and horrible to think of.

OPPOSITE: *Hon. Abraham Lincoln,* lithograph by Currier & Ives, 1860. The "Beardless Lincoln," after a Brady photograph when Lincoln was in New York for his Cooper Union speech of February 27, 1860. His later beard is said to have been in response to a young girl's suggestion that it would improve his appearance. (MCNY)

OPPOSITE: *What Is It?—Or Man Monkey,* lithograph by Currier & Ives, n.d., for "Barnum's Gallery of Wonders, No. 26." An advertisement for the exhibit Strong visited on March 2, 1860. (MCNY)

Other Barnum Wonders: ABOVE: *Vantile Mack, the Infant Lambert, or, Giant Baby!,* lithograph by Currier & Ives, n.d. (MCNY) BOTTOM: *The Maine Giantess—Miss Silva Hardy—Nearly 8 Feet High,* lithograph by Currier & Ives, n.d. (MCNY)

Of course, nobody will be hanged. Somebody has murdered about two hundred people, many of them with hideous torture, in order to save money, but society has no avenging gibbet for the respectable millionaire and homicide. Of course not. He did not want to or mean to do this massacre; on the whole, he would have preferred to let these people live. His intent was not homicidal. He merely thought a great deal about making a large profit and very little about the security of human life. He did not compel these poor girls and children to enter his accursed mantrap. They could judge and decide for themselves whether they would be employed there. It was a matter of contract between capital and labor; they were to receive cash payment for their services. No doubt the legal representatives of those who have perished will be duly paid the fractional part of their week's wages up to the date when they become incapacitated by crushing or combustion, as the case may be, from rendering further service. Very probably the wealthy and liberal proprietor will add (in deserving cases) a gratuity to defray funeral charges. It becomes us to prate about the horrors of slavery! What Southern capitalist trifles with the lives of his operatives as do our philanthropes of the North?

MARCH 2, FRIDAY

Stopped at Barnum's on my way downtown to see the much advertised nondescript, the "What-is-it." Some say it's an advanced chimpanzee, others that it's a cross between nigger and baboon. But it seems to me clearly an idiotic negro dwarf, raised, perhaps, in Alabama or Virginia. The showman's story of its capture (with three other specimens that died) by a party in pursuit of the gorilla on the western coast of Africa is probably bosh. The creature's look and action when playing with his keeper are those of a nigger boy. But his anatomical details are fearfully simian, and he's a great fact for Darwin.

BARNUM'S GALLERY OF WONDERS. Nº 26.

LITH. BY CURRIER & IVES.   Nº — NASSAU ST. N.Y.

WHAT IS IT?—OR "MAN MONKEY".
ON EXHIBITION AT BARNUM'S MUSEUM, NEW YORK.

This is a most singular animal, with many of the features and other characteristics of both the HUMAN and BRUTE species. It was found in Africa, in a perfectly nude state, and with two others captured.— The others died on their passage to this country. At first it ran on all fours, and was with difficulty learned to stand as nearly erect as here represented. It is the opinion of most scientific men that he is a connecting link between the WILD NATIVE
AFRICAN, AND THE ORANG OUTANG.
He is playful as a Kitten and every way pleasing interesting and amusing.
TO BE SEEN AT ALL HOURS.

Broadway, New York, lithograph by Currier & Ives, n.d. This view is to the south, down Broadway from the tip of City Hall Park, sometime in the mid-1850s. On the right is the Astor House, built on the site of John Jacob Astor's home. Next to it is St. Paul's Chapel, where George Washington worshiped in 1789. The next building past the churchyard housed the first daguerreotype studio of Mathew Brady, and in the far distance is the Gothic Revival Trinity Church designed by Richard Upjohn and completed in 1846. On the left side of Broadway is P. T. Barnum's American Museum. (MCNY)

April 13

Heard a good thing of John Van Buren's today.

Scene, Downing's Oyster Cellar. John Van Buren at the counter devouring his shilling's worth of bivalves. Dirty little —, who has recently tried a case with John in which he was beat, and which he made a personal matter against John and John's client, steps up beside him, resolved to say something crushing.

Pettifogger *loquitur*. "Mr. Van Buren, is there any client so dirty that you wouldn't undertake his case?"

John Van Buren (swallows his oyster unmoved and looks over his shoulder at Pettifogger with an expression of concern). "Why, what *have* you been doing?"

Exit Pettifogger. . . .

MAY 19

Thy Nose, O W. H. Seward, is out of joint! The Chicago Convention nominates Lincoln and Hamlin. They will be beat, unless the South perpetrate some special act of idiocy, arrogance, or brutality before next fall.

Lincoln will be strong in the Western states. He is unknown here. The *Tribune* and other papers commend him to popular favor as having had but six months' schooling in his whole life; and because he cut a great many rails, and worked on a flatboat in early youth; all which is somehow presumptive evidence of his statesmanship. The watchword of the campaign is already indicted. It is to be "Honest Abe" (our candidate being a namesake of the Father of the Faithful). Mass-meetings and conventions and committees are to become enthusiastic and vociferous whenever an orator says Abe. But that monosyllable does not seem to me likely to prove a word of power. "Honest Abe" sounds less efficient than "Frémont and Jessie," and that failed four years ago.

The Republican Party Going to the Right House, lithograph by Currier & Ives, 1860. Horace Greeley, editor of the New York *Tribune* is shown "supporting" Abe Lincoln, the "Rail Candidate." Strong points out that the *Tribune* and other papers "commend him to popular favor as having had but six months' schooling in his whole life; and because he cut a great many rails." (MCNY)

The Prince of Wales, lithograph by Currier & Ives, 1860. Strong, on the Reception Committee for the ball honoring the Prince, shook hands with him and wrote that he was thinking of having his "right-hand glove framed and glazed, with an appropriate inscription." (MCNY)

OCTOBER 5

Much occupied with divers matters growing out of the expected advent of our "sweet young Prince." "Long may he wave," but I wish he were at home again with his royal mamma, and I hope the community won't utterly disgrace itself before he goes away. The amount of tuft-hunting and Prince-worshiping threatens to be fearful; and, I don't know how it happens, but I fear my share in the demonstration is to be much larger than I expected or desired. The Reception Committee met today and passed on divers weighty matters. It is proposed that we "wait on the Prince" the evening before the ball, which seems to me a very superfluous work of supererogation. All we can say or do is to express the hope that His Royal Highness finds himself pretty well, considering, and I think His Royal Highness will be inclined to take it for granted that we hope so, whether we call or not.

OCTOBER 11

I begin to be weary of this "sweet young Prince." The Hope of England threatens to become a bore. In fact, he is a bore of the first order. Everybody has talked of nothing but His Royal Highness for the last week. Reaction is inevitable. It has set in, and by Monday next, the remotest allusion to His Royal Highness will act like ipecac. It has been a mild, bland, half-cloudy day. By ten o'clock, people were stationing themselves along the curbstones of Broadway and securing a good place to see the Prince. What a spectacle-loving people we are! Shops were closed and business paralyzed; Wall Street deserted. I spent the morning mostly at the Trinity vestry office, signing tickets, and so forth. We had to pass on a bushel of applications for admission next Sunday. Lots of Fifth Avenueites sent in letters, tendering a private carriage for the conveyance of His Royal Highness to church, with a postscript asking for a "few" tickets. Corporators of Trinity Church bluster about their rights and insist on reserved pews. I fear we are a city of snobs.

OCTOBER 13, SATURDAY

From any more princes of the blood, *libera nos Domine.* May this nice-looking, modest boy find his way home, or at least to our boundaries, with all convenient speed.

I've been in hard work about His Royal Highness for forty-eight hours. I'm weary of His Royal Highness. . . . The Ball is over, thank Heaven, but the Trinity Church reception and services tomorrow are still to be. What they will be, time must tell. I've made the most minute, definite arrangements with Mr. Kennedy and Sergeant Cropsey and the sextons and their aids, but I fear the crowd will out-general me. And I cannot be at the church till the services are actually commencing, for the destinies compel me to accompany or escort the royal party, our guests; and Hyslop and Dunscomb, who will be at the church from nine (when the doors open) till the Prince arrives, are timid and imbecile. I'd give a great deal if tomorrow's august transaction were done and well done.

Mr. Ruggles took Ellie and me, also Mrs. Hunt, to the Astor Library yesterday morning. Only two or three onlookers were present; Mrs. Schuyler and Mrs. John Sherwood. We waited and waited, lounged through alcoves, looked with vain longings at the titles of nice books. The trustees of the library were

The Astor Library of the Present, engraving. Strong "looked with vain longings at the titles of nice books" as he waited for the arrival of the Prince of Wales. (MCNY)

biding their time below, waiting to pounce on His Royal Highness the moment the sound of his chariot wheels should be heard. At length, about eleven o'clock, a noise of much people was heard without—a hooray—an opening of the police-guarded door, feet on the stone staircase, and then a vision of a girlish-looking young boy walking swiftly through the library with Dr. Cogswell, followed by the hairy-faced Duke of Newcastle with Mr. S. B. Ruggles and by William Astor, Carson Brevoort, and others of the library trustees escorting Lord Lyons and a lot of peers and honorables beside. They inspected the premises in double-quick time, and at the head of the staircase on their way out, His Highness shook hands with Cogswell and thanked him very briefly, simply, and nicely, just as any untitled gentleman would have done (think of it!), and the royal party was gone.

At eight to the Academy of Music. The doors were not yet opened to the common herd, but my exalted official position on the committee admitted me by the royal entrance on Fourteenth Street. The house looked brilliant, blazing with lights and decorated with great masses of flowers. My post was with Charles King, Ben Silliman, and Cyrus Field in the room appointed for the reception of invited guests generally. Certain other committees had interfered with our arrangements in an unwarrantable and unconstitutional manner. The consequence of this outrage was (as we had distinctly foreseen and predicted) that

The Auditorium of the Academy of Music, engraving. **Built in 1853-54 on the northeast corner of 14th Street and Irving Place, it was the first opera house to succeed in New York.** *(Ballou's Pictorial Drawingroom Companion)*

the great majority of the invited guests found their way to "the floor" for themselves without being conducted thither by any legitimate organ. Our duties were therefore light. We "received" a few South American and Portuguese diplomats and General Paez and Major Delafield and Captain Cullum and sundry army and navy people and a score of city militia, colonels in most elaborate uniforms, and Mayor Wood (I had a very intimate talk with that limb of Satan); and at ten we adjourned to the special reception room and joined Hamilton Fish and old Pelatiah Perit (who looked like a duke in his dress coat and white cravat), and Peter Cooper, who looked like one of Gulliver's Yahoos caught and cleaned and dressed up.

In came the royal party at last, with the Reception Committeemen, who had been assigned the pleasing duty of escorting them. We were presented to His Royal Highness *seriatim*. I had supposed that shaking hands with a Prince of Wales was indecorous, and that a bow was the proper acknowledgment of introduction to so august a personage; but when the Prince puts out his hand, or extends and proffers his fingers like anybody else, it seems ungracious to decline the honor and say, "Sir, I am so well bred as to know my place, and I am unworthy to shake hands with a descendant of James I and George III and a probable King of England hereafter." I think of having my right-hand glove framed and glazed, with an appropriate inscription.

OCTOBER 31

Republicans refuse to believe secession possible (in which I think they are wrong), and maintain that were it accomplished, it would do us no lasting mischief. I am sure it would do fatal mischief to one section or another and great mischief to both. Amputation weakens the body, and the amputated limb decomposes and perishes. Is our vital center North or South? Which is Body and which is Member? We may have to settle that question by experiment. We are not a polypoid organism that can be converted into two organisms by mere bisection. China is a specimen of that type, but we claim higher rank. Bisection is disaster and degradation, but if the only alternative is everlasting submission to the South, it must come soon, and why should it not come now? What is gained by postponing it four years longer? I feel Republican tonight.

Abraham Lincoln, political engraving.

NOVEMBER 2

Think I will vote the Republican ticket next Tuesday. One vote is insignificant, but I want to be able to remember that I voted right at this grave crisis. The North must assert its rights, now, and take the consequences.

DECEMBER 24

... That termagant little South Carolina has declared herself out of the Union, and resolved to run away and to the sea. How many of the Southern sisterhood will join the secession jig she thus leads off remains to be seen. It strikes me that this proceeding, strictly considered, does not take the soil and the people of South Carolina out of the federal jurisdiction at all, but if it have any legal validity or effect whatever, simply amounts to a resignation of the qualified sovereignty heretofore enjoyed by that state, and converts what was the State of South Carolina into the Territory of South Carolina. It belonged and still belongs to the national government; if it repudiates and resigns the title, duties, and dignity of a state, what can it be but a territory? That its foolish inhabitants want to be called an Empire or a Herzogthum or a Tribe makes no difference.

This proceeding surprises nobody and makes no sensation. It's a grave event, and may well bring tremendous calamity upon the country. It's a grave affair for any family if one of its members goes mad. But as an offset, we have the influx of gold from England and the growing hopes that Northern cities will get through the winter without the panic and crisis and uprising of hungry mobs that our Southern friends complacently predict.

1861

The year that saw the beginning of the Civil War, with the firing on Federal Fort Sumter in Charleston Harbor by Confederate guns in March, found Strong still one of those who would have been willing to pay the price of continued slavery as the price of continued union. But his attitude was to change and become increasingly sympathetic to the plight of blacks. His anger at the seceding states was hardened by the number of Southern sympathizers, "Copperheads," in New York's commercial and professional upper class. Mayor Fernando Wood and Governor Horatio Seymour were among the worst of these.

In the spring, Strong went to Washington to inquire into the wants of the New York regiments stationed in nearby Virginia. There was little fighting as yet, but the disastrous defeat at Bull Run, where the Union troops invading Virginia were driven back in rout to Arlington and Alexandria on the Potomac, was only weeks away.

It was in this year that Strong embarked on the most important civic activity of his life: the formation of the Sanitary Commission, a private organization of prominent citizens deeply concerned over the welfare and health of the rapidly increasing Army. The prime movers were Henry W. Bellows, a Unitarian minister who became its first president; Thomas M. Clark, Episcopal bishop of Rhode Island; Frederick Law Olmsted, the great landscape architect who left his work in Central Park to become general secretary; Charles Janeway Stille, a Philadelphia lawyer who later became the Commission's historian; and Strong himself. The Commission raised vast sums for medical materials and was soon recognized officially by President Lincoln and, much more reluctantly, by Secretary of War Stanton. One of its first jobs was to bring about the removal of an incompetent surgeon-general, a favorite of Stanton's, and to secure the appointment of Dr. William Alexander Hammond.

OVERLEAF: *Bombardment of Fort Sumter, Charleston Harbor*, lithograph by Currier & Ives, n.d. Strong noted on March 15 that "the impression grows stronger that its surrender is unavoidable and that government has not the means to hold it." (MCNY)

FEBRUARY 2

The Rev. Dr. Seabury has put forth a book maintaining the right to hold slaves on religious and ethical principles. It looks sound and sensible. The complaint of Christendom and of all humanity against the South is not founded on their exercise of that right (though most people take for granted that it is a wrong), but on the diabolical peculiarities of the Southern system—separation of families and the like—which I suppose to be mere accidents of slaveholding, not of its essence. . . .

MARCH 5

Weather grows cold again. Much wind and dust. People differ about Lincoln's Inaugural, but favorable criticism preponderates, though stocks have gone down. At Trust Company Board this morning. Kernochan and other ultra "conservative" Southronizers approved and applauded it as pacific and likely to prevent collision. Maybe so, but I think there's a clank of metal in it. It's unlike any message or state paper of any class that has appeared in my time, to my knowledge. It is characterized by strong individuality and the absence of conventionalism of thought or diction. It doesn't run in the ruts of Public Documents, number one to number ten million and one, but seems to introduce one to *a man* and to dispose one to like him. That is its effect on Augustus Clason, for example, a strong Southern Democrat.

The absence of fine writing and spread-eagle-ism is a good sign. Its weak points, I think, are its discussion of the political authority of the Supreme Court of the United States and its admission that the North condemns slaveholding as a moral wrong. That is unfortunate in a paper intended (among other things) to strengthen the hands of Union men at the South. We Northerners object to slavery on grounds of political economy, not of ethics. . . .

MARCH 15

Nothing definite about Fort Sumter, but the impression grows stronger that its surrender is unavoidable and that government has not the means to hold it. Lincoln's Administration cannot fairly be held responsible for this national disgrace. Traitors—Floyd, Cobb, & Co.—have been diligently paralyzing our national strength for months, if not for years. Their successors in office cannot undo the spell at once.

But, whoever may be responsible for the calamity, this is a time of sad humiliation for the country. Every citizen of what has heretofore been called the Great Republic of America, every man, woman, and child, from Maine to Texas, from Massachusetts to California, stands lower among the inhabitants of this earth tonight than in March, 1860. We are a weak divided, disgraced people, unable to maintain our national existence. We are impotent even to *assert* our national life. The country of George Washington and Andrew Jackson (!!!) is decomposing, and its elements reforming into new and strange com-

Confederate recruiting notice, *The Charleston Courier*, September 10, 1861.

binations. I shall never go abroad. That question is settled. I should be ashamed to show my nose in the meanest corner of Europe. Naples and Florence and Milan, now triumphantly asserting their national life and unity, are entitled to look down on Boston and New York. All my right, title, and interest in the Fourth of July and the American Eagle and the Model Republic can be bought at a "low figure."

I'm tempted to emigrate, to become a naturalized British subject and spend the rest of my days in some pleasant sea-side village in the southern counties of old Mother England. It's a pity we ever renounced our allegiance to the British Crown.

APRIL 15

Events multiply. The President is out with a proclamation calling for 75,000 volunteers and an extra session of Congress July 4. It is said 200,000 more will be called within a few days. Every man of them will be wanted before this game is lost and won. Change in public feeling marked, and a thing to thank God for. We begin to look like a United North. Willy Duncan (!) says it may be necessary to hang Lincoln and Seward and Greeley hereafter, but our present duty is to sustain Government and Law, and give the South a lesson. The New York *Herald* is *in equilibrio* today, just at the turning point. Tomorrow it will denounce Jefferson Davis as it denounced Lincoln a week ago. The *Express* is half traitorous and half in favor of energetic action against traitors. The *Journal of Commerce* and the little *Day-Book* show no signs of reformation yet, but though they are contemptible and without material influence for evil, the growing excitement against their treasonable talk will soon make them more cautious in its utterance. The *Herald* office has already been threatened with an attack.

Mayor Wood out with a "proclamation." He must still be talking. It is brief and commonplace, but winds up with a recommendation to everybody to obey the laws of the land. This is significant. The cunning scoundrel sees which way the cat is jumping and puts himself right on the record in a vague general way, giving the least possible offence to his allies of the Southern Democracy. The *Courier* of this morning devotes its leading article to a ferocious assault on Major Anderson as a traitor beyond Twiggs, and declares that he has been in collusion with the Charleston people all the time. This is wrong and bad. It is premature, at least. . . .

APRIL 23

Everyone's future has changed in these six months last past. This is to be a terrible, ruinous war, and a war in which the nation cannot succeed. It can never subjugate these savage millions of the South. It must make peace at last with the barbarous communities off its Southern frontier. I was prosperous and well off last November. I believe my assets to be reduced fifty per cent, at least. But I hope I can still provide wholesome training for my three boys. With that patrimony they can fight out the battle of life for themselves. Their mother is plucky and can stand self-denial. I clearly see that this is a most severe personal calamity to me, but I welcome it cordially, for it has shown that I belong to a community that is brave and generous, and that the City of New York is not sordid and selfish.

JUNE 2, SUNDAY

Drove with Hoffman to Arlington House, the hereditary mansion of that fine old fellow, Colonel [Robert E.] Lee, now unhappily a traitor. A splendid place amid beautiful grounds, through which we strolled a while. The sentinels refused us admission to the house and we were walking back to our carriage when General McDowell came riding up the road with his tail of staff and orderlies. He hailed me, dismounted, took us through the house, and was very kind and obliging. It's a queer place, an odd mixture of magnificence and meanness, like the castle of some illustrious, shabby, semi-insolvent old Irish family; for example, a grand costly portico with half-rotten wooden steps. Hall decorated with pictures, battle-pieces, by some illustrious Custis or other (fearful to behold); also with abundant stags' skulls and antlers.

OPPOSITE: A recruiting station in New York, as illustrated in *Frank Leslie's Illustrated Newspaper.* About 110,000 New York volunteers enlisted in the Union Army. (MCNY)

The Battle of Bull Run, Va., July 21st 1861, lithograph by Currier & Ives, n.d. As in all of this patriotic firm's Civil War battle scenes, the Union troops are victorious; in actuality, they fled the scene in rout at Bull Run. (MCNY)

August 27

It is almost time for another great disaster. It will occur in Western Virginia, probably. Can any disaster and disgrace arouse us fully? Perhaps we are destined to defeat and fit only for subjugation. Perhaps the oligarchs of the South are our born rulers. Northern communities may be too weak, corrupt, gelatinous, and unwarlike to resist Jefferson Davis and his confederates. It is possible that New York and New England and the Free West may be unable to cope with the South. If so, let the fact be ascertained and established as soon as possible, and let us begin to recognize our masters. But I should like a chance to peril my life in battle before that question is decided.

October 12

We had an audience of Lincoln from nine to eleven A.M. Thursday (I think it was Thursday). He is lank and hard-featured, among the ugliest white men I have seen. Decidedly plebeian. Superficially vulgar and a snob. But not essentially. He seems to me clear-headed and sound-hearted, though his laugh is the laugh of a yahoo, with a wrinkling of the nose that suggests affinity with the tapir and other pachyderms; and his grammar is weak. After we had presented our views about the Surgeon-General, and after Lincoln had charged us with "wanting to run the machine" and had been confuted, Bishop Clark introduced the subject of exchange of prisoners. Of course, Lincoln replied that such exchange implied recognition of the rebel government as a legitimate belligerent power, and spoke of the flag of truce sent out to recover Colonel Cameron's body after the battle of Bull Run, and of General Scott's reluctance to send it. The General said he had always held that if he fell in battle, he should be quite satisfied to rest on the battlefield with his soldiers.

Poor old Scott, by the way, is sinking. Grows lethargic, sleeps half the day, and entertains certain jealousies of McClellan. His career is finished. Had a talk with poor McDowell. Still sore and morbid about Bull Run.

General Winfield Scott, **engraving. At the beginning of the Civil War, the Union General-in-Chief was seventy-five years old, weighed 300 pounds, and could not leave his chair unaided.**

1862

Strong had now drastically cut down on his law practice, at considerable cost to his income, and was devoting most of his time to the Sanitary Commission and to his inspection tours, by carriage or hospital ship, to the battlefronts. On May 11 he records his jubilation at the news of Admiral Farragut's destruction of the Confederate gun boat fleet at New Orleans. Musical benefits for the Commission in New York allowed him, even in wartime, to continue his favorite recreation of attending concerts. His disgust with some of his fellow New Yorkers who wanted peace at any price became more and more aggravated. He was one of the founders of the Union League Club that broke off from the Union Club because of the number of Copperheads in the latter.

FEBRUARY 18

Meeting of Executive Committee of Sanitary Commission at Dr. Bellows's at two o'clock. Olmsted with us. We propose now to prepare, at least, to put our house in order, wind up our affairs, and resign. Government keeps no faith with us. From last July till this time, there has been a series of promises unperformed. We got our hospitals erected, to be sure; General Meigs kept his word with us. But that is the single exception. Mr. Secretary Cameron promised and repromised reforms, but nothing was done. McClellan has promised us general orders "this afternoon or tomorrow," begging us always to tell him what we thought necessary at once, but he has issued nary order on our suggestion. So with Lincoln. So with Stanton. It is nearly a month since he pledged himself, with apparent warmth, to decisive steps that have not been taken to this day. We cannot go on asking the community to sustain us with money as an advisory government organ after six months' experience like this. I heartily approve of the proposition to resign. We have been shielding the Medical Bureau all this time from the hurricane of public wrath its imbecility would have raised by our volunteer work. Active operations are beginning now. The Bureau is still imbecile, notwithstanding all our remonstrances. For our own sake, we had better retire and leave the responsibility where it lawfully belongs.

MARCH 12   VIRGINIA

Agnew and Gibbs departed Saturday. On Wednesday, we set forth for Centre-ville and Manassas and Bull Run. The rebels had abandoned the line they held so long. They seem to have begun retreating before we advanced. "The wicked flee when no man pursueth." Warned by the winds of Heaven that were making the roads of Virginia passable, the rebel host had broken up its cantonments and retired across the Rappahannock. Our party was Bellows, Van Buren, Olmsted, Rogers (of Boston, a wealthy stolid citizen who has left his home and taken up his abode in Washington to work for the Commission without pay), Dr. Chamberlain (one of our inspectors) and myself. The expedition took a carriage (driver Uncle Ned, whose services entitle him to the highest com-mendation), three saddle-horses, forage for man and beast, blankets, buffalo robes, and one revolver. We alternated between the carriage and the saddle. Left 244 F Street at eight o'clock in the morning Wednesday and crossed at Aqueduct Bridge. Roads miry and abominable till we struck the Alexandria and Fairfax turnpike. It was a bland, sunny day. Dined at Fairfax Court House al fresco. Great accumulation of troops there. It was far the largest exhibition of war I have yet seen. Camp after camp and long lines of brigade drill, and great columns moving over the dreary hillsides. Thence to Centreville over miry roads. Halted there and set off for Manassas. We got separated by mistake. Olmsted, Chamberlain, and Rogers, the equestrians, took the road to Black-burn's Ford. The rest of us, in the carriage, made for the Stone Bridge, plunging through perilous quagmires and vainly looking for our companions. At Cub Run we found the bridge burned and the ford dangerous in the uncertain evening light. No civilian on horseback had passed that way, as we were assured by certain contrabands [fleeing slaves] marching northwards with bundles on their backs. So we reluctantly and anxiously retraced our steps to Centreville, meeting ghostly looking cavalry pickets going off to their posts over the black plains.

Brookly Sanitary Commission Fair, 1864. Numerous events were held in New York to raise money for helping the wounded, Strong's great pursuit during the Civil War. (MCNY)

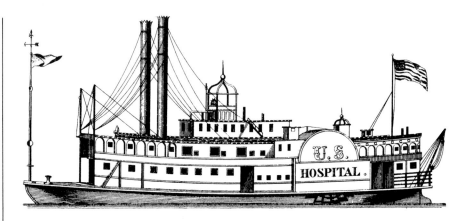

**U.S. Army Hospital Steamer
D. A. January, engraving.**

APRIL 30, WEDNESDAY

Government changed the arrangements for our floating hospital. The steamship, *Daniel Webster*, Captain Bletham, lying at Alexandria, was turned over to us Friday at six o'clock in the morning. She had been used as a transport and was full of filth, had to be thoroughly disinfected and purified and gutted, berths torn down and new ones put up. Gangs of carpenters were sent down to work night and day and a dozen contrabands, supplied by General [James S.] Wadsworth. They attended to the scrubbing and scraping and whitewashing. Spent Saturday morning on board and went down by steam-tug Sunday morning. We were delayed many hours by failure of supplies. Messengers were sent off to ransack Alexandria for fresh meat. They returned at last after an expedition into the back country, and we steamed down the Potomac at four o'clock in the afternoon, passed Mount Vernon and Fort Washington and the Stone Fleet (waiting to be sunk whenever the *Merrimac* shall appear) and anchor off Aquia Creek when daylight fails.

We have on board Olmsted, Agnew, Knapp, Dr. Hartshorne of Philadelphia, Lewis Rutherford, and his son "Stuyvy" (guests of the Commission, as is also that florid and gassy gent, Caleb Lyon "of Lyonsdale"), Stillé of Philadelphia, Mrs. Christine Griffin, Mrs. David Lane, Mrs. Howland, and Miss Woolsey, a dozen he-nurses from Philadelphia, and six or eight nice young medical students from New York, who rank as "dressers." Haight, Woodruff, and Conolly seem very fine, intelligent young fellows; also, Dr. Grymes of Washington, a few officers, and some fifty soldiers. These were government passengers. The soldiers were well behaved and orderly. One of the officers, a chaplain from western New York, Cleveland by name, gave us a "service" Sunday night by invitation, the like of which I do not care to hear again. . . .

Toward four o'clock, we open York river and the gunboats that guard it, and then turn off into "Poquossin" [Pequoson] bay (I am not sure I have got its chivalric name right) and enter Cheeseman's Creek after grounding once or twice. It was a goodly spectacle; a narrow estuary, with low-wooded shores studded with tents and alive with moving masses. Some hundred transports congregated on its still waters—sailing vessels and steamers, big and little, of every degree, some of them black with men of [William B.] Franklin's division, which has now been afloat and waiting for a fortnight. As night came on, all these vessels were lit up, and great campfires glared out on either shore, and there were conflagrations (of brushwood and obstructive timber, probably) that reddened the sky. Men were singing on board the transports, bugle calls and drumbeats were all around, and through these noises came every few minutes the boom of a heavy gun from the lines. These sights and sounds were suggestive.

MAY 11, SUNDAY   NEW YORK

*G*ratias agimus. God be praised for today's news. Did not go out this morning: sent Johnny to St. Paul's with his grandmamma and dawdled over books in the library, and snuffling, snorting, sneezing, and choking with this pestilent cold. Soon after dinner, the streets were full of noises, the cry of panting newsboys with their *extrees.* I posted myself at the front door and discoursed with a patriotic old gentleman who recognized me as an enquirer and imparted the news. I don't know who he was, and it made no difference. We waved our hats to passers-by and they waved theirs. The city was jubilant. At last, a youth came along, and I invested in an extra *Tribune,* declining to receive change for my quarter. Read the news, which I had not dared fully to believe till I saw it in print, and executed a war dance round the hall, to Temple's astonishment.

June 23

Tonight to concert at Academy of Music. It was got up spontaneously by the young men of the Mercantile Society Library for the benefit of the Sanitary Commission. Tolerable house. Guess we shall net $1,000 and upwards. The wonderful Seventh Symphony was on its programme, and of course, covered a multitude of sins—solos, vocal and instrumental, *fioriture,* and bosh. The overtures to *Tannhäuser* and *Euryanthe,* also, are not to be heard every night. The symphony was well enough rendered. Its second movement certainly stands alone, unrivalled in its way, as an expression of hopeless supplication in sorrow, of a despairing cry from the depths and from a horror of great darkness. One might write about it for pages, but what he wrote would be nonsense to everyone but himself, so intangible and incommunicable is the message—addressed by the highest musical art to each individual that feels it. Then that grand, mournful march that comes "sweeping by," like tragedy, "with sceptered pall," silencing the festal phrases of the scherzo; the few massive awful chords that connect these two parts of the third movement, and lead the orchestra back from D major to F; the roaring triumphant chaos and anarchy of the fourth movement. What do they all mean? There must be—or must have been once in Beethoven's heart—a key to this wonderful symphony.

OPPOSITE: **Clinton Hall, on the steps of which Hone witnessed the freeing of a runaway slave on October 27, 1846. He predicted that it was "a trifling incident in the appalling drama which we shall be called to witness, and perhaps bear a part in, during the course of not many years." In Strong's time, Clinton Hall housed the Mercantile Society Library, which sponsored a concert to benefit the Sanitary Commission. (MCNY)**

SEPTEMBER 13

A new and most alarming kind of talk is coming up, emitted by old Breckinridge Democrats (like W. L. Cutting) mostly, and in substance to this effect: "Stonewall Jackson, Lee, and Joe Johnston were all anti-secessionists till the war broke out. No doubt, they still want to see the Union restored. They are personally friends, allies, and political congeners of Halleck, McClellan, F.-J. Porter, and others. Perhaps they will all come together and agree on some compromise or adjustment, turn out Lincoln and his 'Black Republicans' and use their respective armies to enforce their decision North and South and reëstablish the Union and the Constitution." A charming conclusion that would be of our uprising to maintain the law of the land and uphold republican institutions! But we have among us plenty of rotten old Democrats like Judge Roosevelt, capitalists like Joe Kernochan, traders and money dealers like Belmont, and political schemers like James and Rat Brooks, who would sing a *Te Deum* over any pacification, however infamous, and would rejoice to see Jefferson Davis our next President. Perhaps he may be. If he is magnanimous and forgiving he may be prevailed on to come and reign over us. I would rather see the North subjugated than a separation. Disgust with our present government is certainly universal. Even Lincoln himself has gone down at last, like all our popular idols of the last eighteen months. This honest old codger was the last to fall, but he has fallen. Nobody believes in him any more. I do not, though I still maintain him. I cannot bear to admit the country has no man to believe in, and that honest Abe Lincoln is not the style of goods we want just now. But it is impossible to resist the conviction that he is unequal to his place. His only special gift is fertility of smutty stories. *Quam parva sapientia mundus regitur!* What must be the calibre of our rulers whose rule is so disgraceful a failure? If McClellan gain no signal, decisive victory within ten days, I shall collapse; and we have no reason to expect anything of that sort from him.

OCTOBER 3

N ow for my special present aggravation and irritation. The Triennial Convention of the Protestant Episcopal Church in the U.S.A. is now sitting in St. John's Chapel. Mr. Ruggles is a delegate from this diocese. (So is the Rev. F. L. Hawks.) The afternoon papers announce that some Pennsylvania delegate

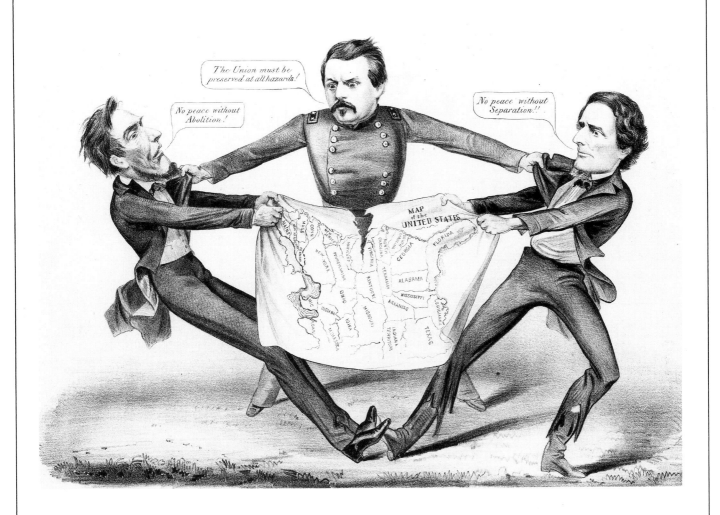

offered a preamble and resolutions in substance that whereas there is a rebellion against the nation and a schism in the church, therefore, resolved that the church prays that the rebels and schismatics may be brought to a better mind, that the bishops be invited to set forth a form of prayer accordingly, and that the church also hopes and prays that the devices of rebellion and schism be confounded. This motion was tabled two to one after full discussion.

The church in which I was brought up, which I have maintained so long to be the highest and noblest of organizations, refuses to say one word for the country at this crisis. Her priests call on Almighty God every day, in the most solemn offices at her liturgy, to deliver His people from "false doctrine, heresy, and schism," from "sedition, privy conspiracy, and rebellion." Now, at last, when they and their people are confronted by the most wicked of rebellions and the most wilful of schisms on the vilest of grounds, the constitutional right to breed black babies for sale, when rebellion and schism are arrayed against the church and against society in the unloveliest form they can possibly assume— the church is afraid to speak. How would she get on were there a large, highly respectable minority sympathizing with adultery, or homicide, or larceny? Alas, for my dreams of twenty years ago!

December 13

Olmsted [Frederick Law] tells me he called on the President the other evening to introduce some ladies (members of his recent "Honorable Convention" from relief societies all over the country), and Abe Lincoln expatiated on this terrible evil. "Order the army to march to any place!" said Abe Lincoln. "Why it's jes' like *shovellin' fleas*. Hee-yah, ya-hah!" Whereupon one of the ladies timidly asked, "Why don't you order stragglers to be *shot*, sir?" and the query not being immediately answered, was repeated. Olmsted says the presidential guffaw died away and the President collapsed and wilted down into an embodiment of everything weak, irresolute, perplexed, and annoyed, and he said, "Oh, I ca-an't do *that*, you know." It's an army of lions we have, with a sheep for commander-in-chief. O for a day of the late Andrew Jackson!

1863

Lord Hartington, the tactless English peer who incurred the wrath of patriots at the Belmont ball, was later to become the eighth duke of Devonshire and to hold portfolios in several of Queen Victoria's ministries.

The year marked the great turning point of the war, with the victories of Vicksburg and Gettysburg, but it was at least partially smeared for Strong by the July riots against the Draft Act in New York, which raged for four days and nights. Irish and other laborers resented the Army regulation that permitted draftees with the cash available to purchase a substitute soldier for $300, and feared the competition for jobs by Negro freedmen coming up from the South. Before the police and regiments returning from victory at Gettysburg had put down the riots, many buildings were burned and some thousand had been killed or wounded.

Throughout the war Strong continued his duties as a trustee of Columbia College and as a vestryman of Trinity Church.

"Cruelty inflicted on Negro boy" during the Draft Riots, as illustrated in *Harper's*. (MCNY)

FEBRUARY 18, WEDNESDAY

I will divert myself by recording the shindy at Belmont's *ballo in maschera* last night, as narrated to me by Charley Strong, an eyewitness thereof. This was one of those stupid, diluted masquerades at which all the women are masked and all the men exposed, like a fleet of old fashioned line-of-battleships encountering a squadron of iron-clads. His *Durchlauchtigkeit* the Marquis of Hartington was there, a gawdy young English swell of the Dundreary type, as I hear, with a lady in domino on his arm (who proved to be that handsome secessionizing Mrs. Yznaga). They stopped to speak to General McClellan, and Charley then observed with amazement that the illustrious lord was parading a showy little *secesh flag,* conspicuously stuck in his buttonhole. After a little polite talk with McClellan, disturbed by no manifestation of disapproval on his part (!), the pair resumed their promenade, and Charley Strong was looking about for Belmont, intending to make representations to him of this impropriety on the part of his guest, when little Johnny Heckscher came along and gave the Marquis a decided jostle or pull, observing at the same time, "It was intentional, sir, quite intentional." The peer said, "Hee-haw-w-w-what's the matter? It's really vewy extawawdinary," and walked on, followed by Heckscher, who repeated his aggressive demonstration, with a like protest against its being supposed an accident, and added, "I want to insult you, sir." The man stammered, decided to leave the lady on his arm in charge of someone else and to go outside the ballroom with Heckscher for an explanation, and Heckscher told him, at last, "If you do not instantly take that thing out of your buttonhole, I'll pull it out." So Great Britain took it out and put it in its pocket, and (I'm told) apologized to Heckscher afterwards, very frankly, on the ground of ignorance and absence of intention to offend. Good for Heckscher, and not very bad for the young Englisher, who had been consorting with W. Duncan and Belmont and naturally thought sympathy with rebellion *the thing* in New York.

JULY 19, SUNDAY

Have been out seeking information and getting none that is to be trusted. Colonel Frank Howe talks darkly and predicts an outbreak on the east side of the town tonight, but that's his way. I think this Celtic beast with many heads is driven back to his hole for the present. When government begins enforcing the draft, we shall have more trouble, but not till then.

Not half the history of this memorable week has been written. I could put down pages of incidents that the newspapers have omitted, any one of which would in ordinary times be the town's talk. Men and ladies attacked and plundered by daylight in the streets; private houses suddenly invaded by gangs of a dozen ruffians and sacked, while the women and children run off for their lives. Then there is the unspeakable infamy of the nigger persecution. They are the most peaceable, sober, and inoffensive of our poor, and the outrages they have suffered during this last week are less excusable—are founded on worse pretext and less provocation—than St. Bartholomew's or the Jew-hunting of the Middle Ages. This is a nice town to call itself a centre of civilization! Life and personal property less safe than in Tipperary, and the "people" (as the *Herald* calls them) burning orphan asylums and conducting a massacre. How this infernal slavery system has corrupted our blood, North as well as South! There should be terrible vengeance for these atrocities, but McCunn, Barnard & Co. are our judges and the disgrace will rest upon us without atonement.

"Rioters pillaging Colored Orphan Asylum" during the Draft Riots, as depicted in *Harper's*. "This is a nice town to call itself a centre of civilization!" Strong writes, "the 'people' (as the *Herald* calls them) burning orphan asylums and conducting a massacre." (MCNY)

"Rioters hanging Negro and burning his body" during the **Draft Riots,** as shown in *Harper's.* (MCNY)

I am sorry to find that England is right about the lower class of Irish. They are brutal, base, cruel, cowards, and as insolent as base. Choate (at the Union League Club) tells me he heard this proposition put forth by one of their political philosophers in conversation with a knot of his brethren last Monday: "Sure and if them dam Dutch would jine us we'd drive the dam Yankees out of New York entirely!" These caitiffs have a trick, I hear, of posting themselves at the window of a tenement house with a musket, while a woman with a baby in her arms squats at their feet. Paddy fires on the police and instantly squats to reload, while Mrs. Paddy rises and looks out. Of course, one can't fire at a window where there is a woman with a child!! But how is one to deal with women who assemble around the lamp-post to which a Negro had been hanged and cut off certain parts of his body to keep as souvenirs? Have they any womanly privilege, immunity, or sanctity?

No wonder St. Patrick drove all the venomous vermin out of Ireland! Its biped mammalia supply that island its full average share of creatures that crawl and eat dirt and poison every community they infest. Vipers were superfluous. But my own theory is that St. Patrick's campaign against the snakes is a Popish delusion. They perished of biting the Irish people.

AUGUST 11

We hardly appreciate, even yet, the magnitude of this war, the issues that depend on its result, the importance of the chapter in the world's history that we are helping to write. In our hearts we esteem the struggle as the London *Times* does, or pretends to. God forgive our blindness! It is the struggle of two hostile and irreconcilable systems of society for the rule of this continent. Since Mahometanism and Christendom met in battle this side the Pyrenees, there has been no struggle so momentous for mankind. I think that Grant and Rosecrans, Lee and Stonewall Jackson and Joe Johnston, and all the others, will be more conspicuous and better known to students of history A.D. 1963 than Wallenstein and Gustavus, Condé, Napoleon, Frederick, Wellington, and the late Lord Raglan; not as greater generals, but as fighting on a larger field and in a greater cause than any of them. So will our great-great-grandchildren look back on them a century hence, whatever be the result.

DECEMBER 7

Cold for the season. Exceedingly busy all day. Columbia College trustees met at two. Committee on the Course reported. Their resolution to maintain a separate chair of physics passed *sub silentio,* and that of abolishing the calculus and higher analytical geometry (or rather, making them optional in the senior year) after a lively and really very able debate. Rutherfurd and Bradford supported it and Anderson opposed. He lost his temper just a little for the first time in his life, probably, said we were "making the physical course a farce," and got gently snubbed therefor by Bradford. It's very strange, but though Anderson is a man of great and varied acquirements, speaking with the authority of an expert on many subjects, personally most genial, kindly, and lovable, and endowed with the most subtle faculty of argumentation, he has less weight and influence in the board than any other of its members. . . .

1864

Giulian Verplanck, founder of the Century Club, and the defeated Whig candidate for mayor of New York in 1834, was a lovable and highly respected old gentleman, but his persistent tolerance for all things Southern at length outraged his fellow members. Strong's February 24 entry graphically illustrates the swing of public opinion to an unforgiving condemnation of the Confederacy.

The Mrs. S. G. Howe he speaks of on February 6 was Julia Ward Howe, author of the "Battle Hymn of the Republic," which was written after a visit to an Army camp in 1861. Charles Sumner was the abolitionist Massachusetts senator whose caning on the floor of the Senate by a kinsman of a Southern congressman in 1856 created widespread fury in the North.

Secretary of War Stanton's opposition to Dr. William Alexander Hammond as surgeon-general led ultimately to the latter's discharge. Hammond had replaced one of Stanton's favorites, and the secretary tended to regard all who were not with him on any point as his personal enemies, which is why he gave Strong, a Hammond supporter, such a hard time.

General Grant was fighting that summer to reach the James River below Richmond and to establish a base where he could be supplied by sea for a march on the Confederate capital. In one month, Grant's army lost nearly 60,000 men, roughly the equivalent of Lee's entire command, but on May 11 he had notified Army Chief of Staff Henry W. Halleck that he proposed "to fight it out along this line if it takes all summer." Strong visited him during this campaign, taking with him his thirteen-year-old son Johnny.

JANUARY 9

Nothing noteworthy at No. 823 this afternoon. At Century Club tonight was the annual election and a great crowd; one hundred and seventy-six votes polled, an unprecedented number. It was understood this morning that Verplanck had been advised by his friends not to run and had decided to decline a reëlection. But unfortunately for him and for his personal friends like myself, he did not so decide, so I had to vote against him. The result was Verplanck 61, Bancroft 110, scattering 5. Considering Verplanck's popularity and his long identification with the Club, and Bancroft's foibles and snobbishness, this is an encouraging sign. Twenty people said to me tonight, in substance: "How unpleasant it is to vote for a snob like Bancroft, and against my old friend Verplanck! But Verplanck's Copperhead talk is intolerable." I think our Union League Club has done something toward educating people's moral sense up to this point.

Verplanck means to be and tries to be a loyal, patriotic citizen, after his kind. But he is naturally incapable of warm, hearty, generous impulses, except in his personal relations, and (like the Bourbons) he "learns nothing and forgets nothing." He does not see how times have changed and how fast they are changing. He looks on the great national movement that is growing stronger every day and already controls the conduct of the war just as he looked on the ravings of the little knot of philanthropes and infidels that constituted the Abolition Society twenty-five years ago.

FEBRUARY 6

...Story of Mrs. S. G. Howe, [author of] *Passion Flowers,* inviting the Hon. Charles Sumner to dinner "to meet" certain notables of lower grade than his own. Sumner responds languidly that he has been engrossed so long by grand public questions that he has quite lost all interest in individuals. Mrs. Howe replies that she is glad to hear of his progress, for the Almighty has not reached that point *yet*.

FEBRUARY 24

The change of opinion on this slavery question since 1860 is a great historical fact, comparable with the early progress of Christianity and of Mahometanism. Who could have predicted it, even when the news came that Sumter had fallen, or even a year and a quarter afterwards, when Pope was falling back on Washington, routed and disorganized? I think this great and blessed revolution is due, in no small degree, to A. Lincoln's sagacious policy. But I do wish A. Lincoln told fewer dirty stories. What a marvellous change it is! Henry Clitz, Walter Cutting, and Jem Ruggles avowing themselves damn Abolitionists, and my little Louis singing after dinner, Sundays: "John Brown's bodies lies a-modrin' in the graves" just as if it were "The Star-Spangled Banner." Abolitionism established in the District of Columbia, and triumphantly rampant under state laws in Maryland and Missouri! *Mirifica Opera Tua.* God pardon our blindness of three years ago! But for our want of eyes to see and of courage to say what we saw, the South would never have ventured on rebellion.

FEBRUARY 27

Daniel Lord stopped me in Wall Street this morning to tell me how delighted he was to learn that I was to succeed King as President of Columbia College!!! He would accept no denial of his premises and said sundry things that were gratifying when said by so sharp a censor of men and things as Daniel Lord.

From all I hear about the views expressed by Anderson, King, John Astor, William Schermerhorn, and other trustees, I incline to think a majority of the board would put me into that place, marvellous as such action would be, provided I would consent to emigrate from 74 East Twenty-first Street to a frontier settlement in the "President's House" on Forty-ninth Street, where Ellie would be a mile away from all her friends, and the three boys as far from their schools, and all four in peril of typhus and malarial fever, as the vacant blocks of that region are dug up for improvement during the next ten years. That is among the things I will not do on any terms.

MAY 6, FRIDAY   WASHINGTON, D.C.

I spent mostly in letter writing. At half-past nine in the evening, Agnew and I went to Governor (now Senator) Morgan's by appointment, and with him to the War Department for an interview with Secretary Stanton. Our object was to tell that terrible Turk in substance this: "Mr. Secretary, the Committee will have x plus y dollars to spend for the aid and relief of your army and the promotion of its efficiency during the campaign now just opened. Your cordial sympathy and cooperation will add fifty per cent to the value and effect of every dollar we spend. We know we do not enjoy the light of your favor; on the contrary, quite the reverse. You habitually denounce us and our work, and commonly talk of the Commission as a 'swindling concern.' Will you please tell us what you mean by it, why you hate us, and what we can do to appease your august disapprobation and secure for our unpaid, unofficial, unrecognized private exertions for the benefit of your army the neutrality—at least—of the War Department?"

After a little dangling in the antechamber, where we discoursed with Chauncey McKeever, General Augur, and Senator Harris, we "sailed in" to run Stanton's batteries under protection and convoy of Morgan, who had no occasion, however, to "shell the woods" or gun-fire at all during our two hours session. Our reception was on the whole rather grim, such as a medieval saint would have vouchsafed to the Devil on receiving a call from that functionary. We presented the resolution of the Commission appointing a committee to wait on the Secretary, on hearing which the Secretary remarked, "Well, Sir???" Agnew proceeded thereupon to state from memoranda he had prepared an outline of our work and our expenditure, which Stanton interrupted with inexpressible venom and viciousness of manner. "I don't perceive any mention here of what you must have paid for your scurrilous attacks on me and on the Administration through the public press." We could not guess what he meant, and I humbly asked for light. We found that he referred to an article in an early number of the *Bulletin* (signed "A Republican"), urging that the Surgeon-General ought not to be displaced without a court-martial or an investigation in some form. We submitted that this article discussed fairly and temperately a question bearing directly on the efficacy of the medical service and reminded him that it simply recommended him to do what he did a month afterwards. Then he brought up the memorable circular of last January. We said this was no act of the Commission, and that the Commission was in no way responsible for it. But Stanton said he had proof that it had been laid on the desks of members of Congress by "our agent in Washington"—as to which fact we had no knowledge and could say nothing. He dwelt with ferocious delight on the disgraceful conduct of Peirce, Agassiz, and Hill, "whose signatures had been *fraudulently obtained*"—by whom he couldn't say.

It occurred to both Agnew and myself to tell him of the affidavits now in New York, describing the deliberate reading of that paper and the careful consideration of its purport, after which these gentlemen signed it, but it also occurred to us both that it would be unwise to shew our hand, and inexpedient to waste time in a squabble about details. So we took the Secretary's fire with serenity, and his manner became less insolent when he found we were not much frightened. Then he attacked our pension and back-pay system as not within our proper sphere, but this position (though his only strong one) he finally abandoned, admitting that the work was useful and important, forced upon us in a manner, and subject only to a technical objection.

Next came a savage assault on our hospital supply system, kept up at Washington during the past year (but now wound up, I'm happy to say). "We had gone into the marketing business and made ourselves a trading association. Hammond's order that surgeons get their extra supplies through this channel was a gross violation of law, because all purchases were required to be by contract." There we *had* him. It was clear that the Secretary of War didn't know what a "Hospital Fund" is, or the regulations applicable to its disbursement.

We enlightened him on this subject. He gasped and staggered, but soon came up again, and insinuated rather than asserted that the Commission had made money by the operation. "On the contrary, Mr. Secretary, our books and vouchers shew a balance against us of from $5,000 to $10,000." Whereupon the Secretary hit out viciously, but rather wild. "Then that amount of money has been lost—so much of the people's bounty wasted in this job." Our answer was obvious. This balance represents so much contributed to the hospitals, just as directly and effectually as if it had been used to buy them its equivalent in chickens, fresh eggs, and butter. The Commission has turned over the stores it bought and charged the hospital fund their cost price and no more, thus saving that fund not merely the profit of the middleman but also the expense of transportation. Of course the Secretary saw this, but he did not choose to say so, and changed the subject.

Agnew, who showed great tact, temper, and presence of mind throughout, said: "Well, Mr. Secretary, these criticisms are, after all, just what we have long wished to have the Department give us. What we want is the establishment of such relations with you as will secure our receiving your views and suggestions from time to time, and we shall, of course, and so on, always listen to your advice with—and so on." But this was among the things Stanton did not happen to want, and he withdrew himself at once, like a startled land-tortoise, or an irritated actinia. "You must execute your great trust in your own way, and on your own responsibility. I cannot advise you about it." So our interview ended at last, the Secretary taking leave of us with more civility than he had previously shewn.

JULY 1, FRIDAY   VIRGINIA

Up at daybreak with Johnny and Dr. McDonald and up the river by the *City of Troy,* leaving the *Commander* in charge of Lord to turn over the contents of her lower hold to the *Elizabeth* and then return to New York for another cargo of pickles and onions and curried cabbage. Most sultry. Below Harrison's Landing, where a force of cavalry raiders lately crossed, the air is black with innumerable turkey-buzzards; indeed, these foul birds are visible everywhere on the banks of the James River. Pass the rebel *Atlanta,* now converted into a loyal iron-clad, lying off Fort Powhatan. She looks like an ugly customer. City Point at nine. The waters swarming with transports, hospital boats, tugs, gunboats, and light steamers and all manner of river craft. Land in a scene of

OPPOSITE: *Battle of Spottsylvania, Va., May 12th 1864,* lithograph by Currier & Ives, n.d. Spottsylvania was one of a series of drawn-out battles in which Lee prevented Grant from reaching Richmond. Between the time of this battle and when Strong visited him, Grant had lost nearly 60,000 men—roughly equivalent to Lee's entire command. (MCNY)

matchless dust, confusion (apparent at least), and activity. They are repairing the railroad. Wagon trains are moving every way. Gangs of contrabands following mounted leaders who carry remarkably long riding whips—(*honi soit qui mal y pense*); docks are being built, officers riding about, and the usual nebula of stragglers, disabled men, and army followers is all-pervading. Everyone desperately in earnest about something. The shore is lined three deep, yes, six deep, with barges, and the like, steamers are screeching, corrals of mules braying—but I can do no justice to the sights and sounds of the place. All this is on or beside a strip of river shore. Back of this is a bank covered with fine trees and shrubs that were green once, but are now ash-colored and gray. Among them are tents of the same neutral tint. To your right, on the bank, there is a refreshing bit of warm color, the flag of Grant's headquarters. Looking still farther, you make out dimly through the yellow dust-saturated air the outline of a long series of pavilion hospitals, where 6,000 sick and wounded men (too sorely hurt or too ill to be on transportation) are stifling as they breathe the sluggish, heavy current of dust that keeps pouring in upon them. High up against the blue sky stand great columns of coppery dust, hardly moving and shifting their vague outlines slowly, like thunderheads as a storm blows up.

Landing Supplies on the James River, **photograph by Mathew Brady, c. 1861. (LC)**

Join Agnew, and proceed at once to our headquarters (Sanitary Commission); sundry barges moored on the mud-bank of the shore, a festering expanse of filthiness. In all respects a most insanitary arrangement. Our men are so full of their work that they neglect themselves. No wonder more than twenty of our relief corps have broken down and gone home within so short a space. There is everything to produce disease, not only in their work, but in their food and quarters. It is disgraceful and murderous. We gave Douglass (in charge) our views about it, and shall do so formally in writing, with definite orders for reform so far as reform is possible. The situation is bad enough *per se* and cannot be changed at present, but precautions can be taken against disease—and there are none now. The Sanitary Commission needs a new Sanitary Commission to look after the health of its small army of field agents, and our Executive Committee must undertake the work instanter.

With Agnew to Grant's headquarters, taking Johnny with us that he might enjoy a sight of *the* great man of the day—perhaps of the age. Heaven grant it! Headquarters camp is pleasantly situated on top of the bluff, among fine old trees, near the house of a runaway rebel named Eppes. Ingalls has set up his quartermastering offices in the building. It has been riddled and made nearly untenantable by shot and shell, having been used as a trap to decoy some of our men under fire by a story of some sick lady in it who wanted the attendance of a surgeon from our fleet. Such is the story. Ingalls had three little niggers fanning him and looked like a Rajah.

Call on Captain Jones, General Rawlins (chief of staff), and to General Grant's tent. Most cordially received. Talk with him about transportation of vegetables to the front, and so on. He's a man of few words, but gave us clearest assurance of his readiness to help our work, and of his intelligent recognition of its importance. Whenever we want facilities of any kind, we must come straight to him, or send Dr. Douglass, and he will "see us through." Our discourse lasted some fifteen minutes. We made it as brief as possible, though the General professed to be quite disengaged. The impression he makes on me is favorable. He talks like an earnest business man, prompt, clear-headed, and decisive, and utters no bosh. As we were leaving, something was said about encouraging enlistments, and the need of more men. "I think we shall want more men," said Grant, "but there will be no difficulty in getting them."

1865

The surrender of the Confederate forces at Appomattox on April 9 was followed less than a week later by the assassination of President Lincoln. "Up with the black flag now!" Strong dolefully records. The conspirators in the assassination plot were tried by a military commission that was guilty of grave procedural errors, though a fair trial in that day of inflamed feelings probably could not have been obtained. Four were sentenced to death and hanged: George Atzerodt, for the attempted murder of Vice President Andrew Johnson; Lewis Payne, for the attempted murder of Secretary of State William H. Seward; David Herrold, for aiding the foiled escape of the actual assassin, John Wilkes Booth (tracked down and killed nearly two weeks later), and Mary Surratt, who kept the boarding house where the conspirators met.

This year of triumph and tragedy ended with Strong's dinner party in New York for General and Mrs. Grant.

APRIL 15, SATURDAY

Nine o'clock in the morning. *LINCOLN AND SEWARD ASSASSINATED LAST NIGHT!!!!*

The South has nearly filled up the measure of her iniquities at last! Lincoln's death not yet certainly announced, but the one o'clock despatch states that he was then dying. Seward's side room was entered by the same or another assassin, and his throat cut. It is unlikely he will survive, for he was suffering from a broken arm and other injuries, the consequence of a fall, and is advanced in life. Ellie brought this news two hours ago, but I can hardly *take it in* even yet. *Eheu* A. Lincoln!

I have been expecting this. I predicted an attempt would be made on Lincoln's life when he went into Richmond; but just now, after his generous dealings with Lee, I should have said the danger was past. But the ferocious malignity of Southerners is infinite and inexhaustible. I am stunned, as by a fearful personal calamity, though I can see that this thing, occurring just at this time, may be overruled to our great good. Poor Ellie is heartbroken, though never an admirer of Lincoln's. We shall appreciate him at last.

Up with the Black Flag now!

Ten P.M. What a day it has been! Excitement and suspension of business even more general than on the 3rd instant. Tone of feeling very like that of four years ago when the news came of Sumter. This atrocity has invigorated

The Assassination of President Lincoln. At Ford's Theater, Washington, D.C., April 14th 1865, lithograph by Currier & Ives, 1865. (MCNY)

OVERLEAF: *The Funeral of President Lincoln, New York, April 25th, 1865,* lithograph by Currier & Ives, 1865. **The cortege turns at the top of Union Square.** (MCNY)

national feeling in the same way, almost in the same degree. People who pitied our misguided brethren yesterday, and thought they had been punished enough already, and hoped there would be a general amnesty, including J. Davis himself, talk approvingly today of vindictive justice and favor the introduction of judges, juries, gaolers, and hangmen among the dramatis personae. Above all, there is a profound, awe-stricken feeling that we are, as it were, in immediate presence of a fearful, gigantic crime, such as has not been committed in our day and can hardly be matched in history.

June 8

At 823 today was an Andersonville prisoner, who said he had seen his brethren there on their hands and knees around the latrines of that infernal pen, grubbing among faeces for undigested beans and grains of corn wherewith to mitigate the pains of slow starvation.

June 20

Next session of Congress will be an anxious time. "Darkey Suffrage" is a dark and troublesome question, and it must be met. That freedmen, who have as a class always helped the national cause to the utmost of their ability, at risk of their lives, should have political rights at least equal to those of the bitter enemies of the country who are about to resume those rights, sullenly and under protest, only because they are crushed, coerced, and subjugated, is (abstractly considered) in the highest degree just and right. But the average field hand would use political power as intelligently as would the mule he drives. The current phrase that "those who have helped the country with bullets should be permitted to help it with ballots" is mere nonsense. . . . Were I President, I should aim at securing political rights to property-holding Ethiopians and to such as could read and write.

June 28

To Columbia College Commencement at the Academy of Music. Discoursed with sundry agreeable people in the reception room, and then marched in august procession down the parquet with Barnard and the faculty and Fish and Governor Morgan, and the other fashionables, to the sound of soft music, and took my seat on the stage. Sat through six or eight orations and poems. I will not answer for the Greek and Latin salutatories, but all the rest were very small trash, and the efforts of the poets to be smart and funny would have given a cassowary the dyspepsia. . . . There should be a stern censorship of Commencement speeches. The only decent thing I heard was Mendelssohn's exquisite little melody, "Ich wollt' mein Lieb ergöss sich," rendered by a most respectable orchestra—an improvement on the Commencement brass bands of my college days. As each orator made his final bow, there came a concentric fire of bouquets from all parts of the house. The fair artillerists sometimes made bad practice. A four-pound bouquet hit me on the leg, and a ten-pounder took the Rev. Morgan Dix in the eye, producing a contusion of the left spectacle. When the cannonade ceased, the orators gathered up these graceful tributes and carried them off, and then came back for a second armful, looking like "Posy John," the peripatetic florist of Broadway. This absurd practice ought to be stopped somehow. The graduating class appeared in academic head-gear, "Oxford caps," for the first time. On the whole, I thought what I heard of these "commencement exercises" no credit to the College, but rather a lamentable proof that we, the trustees, are doing our duty most imperfectly. . . .

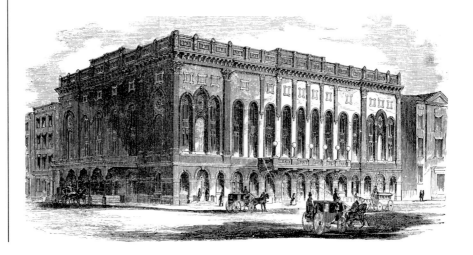

The Academy of Music, engraving, 1856. (Ballou's Pictorial Drawingroom Companion)

July 7

Extr-r-r-y *Times* this afternoon (our first extra for two months, I think) announced that Payne & Co., Mrs. Surratt included, had been duly and decorously hanged. That word *extra* has been a word of power all through these four years. How many scores or hundreds of times has the suspicion of its distant sound started me up from this very desk, at midnight or later, and sent me down stairs to unlock the front door and stand outside, in hope of waylaying a circumambient newsboy. How often have I jumped up spasmodically, saying to Ellie, "There's an extra," and rushed off to secure it. And what a bad article of news I often got. . . .

People seem better satisfied with the findings of the Military Commission than I thought they would be. The feeling seems general that the four who were capitally convicted and whose sentence is now executed got no more than they deserved. There are a few to whom hanging a woman (Mrs. Mary E. Surratt) is rather distasteful, but it troubles them little. Killing women is certainly an unpleasant office, but if a man and a woman be both guilty of murder, the woman deserves the severer punishment. The depravity that produced the crime must be presumed greater in her case, because it had to overcome and outweigh the instincts of her womanly nature. . . .

OPPOSITE: *Hanging at Washington Arsenal; Hooded Bodies of Four Conspirators,* photograph by Alexander Gardner, July 7, 1865. The body of Mrs. Mary E. Surratt at left, her skirts decorously tied at the knees for modesty's sake. Strong noted that "killing women is certainly an unpleasant office, but . . . the depravity that produced the crime must be presumed greater in her case, because it had to overcome and outweigh the instincts of her womanly nature." (LC)

SEPTEMBER 8

I forgot to note the other evening a part of that wicked little Mrs. LeRoy's recent experiences. Major-General C. had been making fierce love to her and supposed himself accepted, though the position to which he aspired had been vacated by the death of poor Bob hardly six months ago. So he proceeded to Point Judith, bringing with him cases of champagne, baskets of fruit, and no end of pâtés and the like from Duncan's. The first evening after his arrival at Anthony's, the lovely widow committed some little sin against the conventionalities that rather offended the general's nice sense of propriety. He told his beloved not to do so any more, and the lady responded by denying his right to any control over her conduct. This led to an explanation, and a disillusionation, and a treaty of mutual secession. One of its clauses provided for the destruction by fire of all the general's amatory epistles—a rather bulky mass of MS. They thought it would attract attention if they went into Anthony's kitchen and poked the bundle of letters into the range, and decided to burn them in some out-of-the-way place on the beach—"by the sad seawaves"—next morning. So off they went, after breakfast (the general in white pantaloons and lemon-colored kids, with his pockets full of locofoco matches), selected a convenient locality for the holocaust, and proceeded to inaugurate that ceremonial. But the wind was high and the sea air damp. They scraped match after match, but not one would ignite, or keep ignited long enough to do its office. The general, however, found a newspaper in his pocket, and they went into a bathing house, whence they emerged, each with a paper torch lit up within its shelter. They fired their pile of amatory epistolography and watched its burning. While it burned, a lot of boys and men came down to go a-clamming or a-fishing and asked whether that was a clam-bake, and two ladies appeared and took possession of the bathing house, proposing to disrobe themselves for a saltwater dip. The lovers—or ex-lovers—watched the blazing pyre till it burned out. Then they suddenly perceived that they had set the beach grass on fire and that the conflagration was fast approaching the bathing house and its disrobing inmates. Mrs. LeRoy tired to put it out. She couldn't do it. She invoked the aid of her adorer. He said, "I can't. I shall black my pantaloons." So the lady rushed into the bathing house and borrowed a pail and invoked the assistance of the clam-diggers. Between them they put out the fire. Her lover watched the process and said, "Good God, what a position for a major-general of the U.S.A.!" and went off by the next train.

Ulysses S. Grant, **carte-de-visite as president. (MCNY)**

NOVEMBER 17

General Grant is to dine here tomorrow with his staff, and I feel quite nervous about so august a transaction.

NOVEMBER 18

Our symposium did not go into operation till half-past six, for the Lieutenant-General and his staff were behind time like Grouchy at Waterloo. Grant appeared at last, however, with Mrs. Grant and with General Comstock, Colonel Badeau, and Colonel Babcock of his staff. I made it a point to have Johnny, Temple, and Louis present, and to bring them severally up to shake hands with the General. They will remember it fifty years hence, if they live so long, and tell their children of it, if they ever have any. Mrs. Ellie had organized her dinner table thus:

Mrs. George T. Strong

Gen. Grant	Sen. Foster of Conn.
Mex. Gen. or Señor Romero	Mrs. Morgan
Mrs. Gen. Grant	Henry J. Raymond
Mr. S. B. Ruggles	Col. Babcock
Gov. Morgan	Mrs. Dix
Gen. Dix	Col. Badeau
Mrs. Ruggles	Chas. Bristed
Gen. Comstock	Mrs. Foster

Egomet Ipsissimus

It was a brilliant, distinguished, or "nobby" assemblage, and they all seemed to have a pleasant time, as people always do at any party organized by Mistress Ellen. I must say that I think it a great honor and privilege to have received Grant here, and there is no element of snobbishness in my feeling about it. We owe the privilege to Ellie's attractions and tact: Foster took her to call on Mrs. Grant, who was much delighted with her, and asked her to lend her aid and countenance to the reception at the Fifth Avenue Hotel Monday night. Ellie slipped in an invitation to dinner, and it was cordially accepted. William B. Astor's was declined, but I am verging on snobbery.

1866–1867

Strong had now returned to the full-time practice of law. In February he argued his first case before the Supreme Court. The case was Society for Savings *v.* Coite, in which Strong's client challenged the constitutionality of a state tax on Federal securities held by state banks.

Strong began by sympathizing with President Andrew Johnson in his struggle with the Republican radicals in Congress, led by Charles Sumner and Thaddeus Stevens, who wished to keep bludgeoning the stricken South, but Johnson's uncouth public appearances at length disgusted him.

Andrew Johnson, carte-de-visite as president. Strong wrote that until the summer of 1866, he held "A. Johnson among the greatest and best of men." (MCNY)

1866

FEBRUARY 10

I have seen the face of the Supreme Court of the United States and live (though with a slight headache). . . . At eleven o'clock, there was the voice of one crying: "The Honorable Chief Justice and the Associate Justices of the Supreme Court of the United States!" Mr. Chief Justice Chase and his associates in their judicial robes marched solemnly into the courtroom, everyone rising. The Court bowed to the Bar, and *vice-versa,* and the crier "made an oyez," finishing it off with "God save the United States of America and this Honorable Court!" I wish more of these Old World formalities survived among us. Judge Allen then moved my admission as attorney and counselor of the Court, and "introduced me." I bowed, and was bowed to by the Bench, took the usual oath in the courtroom (that I would demean myself decently as an officer of the Court and obey its directions), and then went to the Clerk's office and took the special "iron-clad" oath that I had never designedly given Rebellion any aid or comfort, which oath I took most honestly and heartily, with no mental reservation whatever—thank God.

Then the Court proceeded to hear the "Bankers and Brokers Cases" under the Internal Revenue Act. . . .

I hoped the defense would keep the Court occupied till the hour of adjournment. But I saw the Attorney-General was beginning to run emptiness and would soon dry up. I was sickening for a lunch after my early breakfast; was faint and heart-sunken. My hopes were in vain. The Attorney-General sat down at two o'clock, the Chief Justice bowed toward me, by way of invocation, and I got on my legs as one gets into a cold plunge bath. Once up—the ice broken—I was self-possessed and comfortable, and trotted out my little notions and lectured the Supreme Court "like a Dutch uncle" (why Dutch?). I was heard with the utmost courtesy and attention. Court adjourned at three P.M. On the Capitol stairs I crossed Judge Nelson diagonally and took off my hat. He stopped me most kindly, shook hands, introduced me to Judge Clifford, said sundry civil things, and as we parted remarked *sotto voce,* "I think you were a little nervous when you *began* your argument, Mr. Strong, but you will be all right tomorrow morning."

In fact, I was not nervous or alarmed. I was merely suffering physical depression for want of an oyster or two. But how kind this was of old Nelson; how good in the learned old judge to think of an encouraging word for the goose and greenhorn of an advocate! We generally forget the importance and value of such kind offices. This makes me Nelson's backer and supporter to my life's end!

AUGUST 6, MONDAY

Cholera multiplies. Cases are confined as yet to our disgraceful tenement houses and foul side streets—filthy as pigsties and even less wholesome. The epidemic is God's judgment on the poor for neglecting His sanitary laws. It will soon appear as His judgment on the rich for tolerating that neglect—on landlords for poisoning the tenants of their unventilated, undrained, sunless rookeries, poisoning them as directly as if the landlord had put a little ratsbane into the daily bread of each of the hundred families crowded within the four walls of his pest-house. And the judgment will be not on the owners of tenement houses alone, but on the whole community. It is shameful that men, women, and children should be permitted to live in such holes as thousands of them occupy this night in this city. We are letting them perish of cholera and then (as Carlyle suggests somewhere) they will prove their brotherhood and common humanity by killing us with the same disease—that capacity of infection being the only tie between us that we could not protest against and decline to recognize.

Strong ironically identifies the growing cholera epidemic as "God's judgment on the poor for neglecting His sanitary laws." And yet, men, women, and children are so desperate that they must scavenge garbage for anything edible or of value. This engraving appeared within six weeks of Strong's August 6 entry. (*Harper's*)

SEPTEMBER 14

Visit from Dr. Peters this evening. He says that French physicians recognize a disease which they call the "malady of forty years." It attacks, Dr. Peters says, men who had led a dull, monotonous-lifed routine. They suddenly or gradually lose vital force and get somehow all wrong. This disease is partly physical, partly mortal. Its only remedy is total change of scene and atmosphere. So Peters says I *must* go abroad, or go somewhere out of New York for a few months. He guarantees that I will come back fresh as a daisy, and as good as new. His prescription is pleasant, but he might as well advise me to jump over the City Hall. I am not in funds for a foreign tour.

OCTOBER 9

...No news yet from Pennsylvania or from any of the state elections of today. We shall know something of their result tomorrow morning. God send us good news. If the country would avoid ruin it must sternly repudiate A. Johnson and his "policy." To that conclusion have I come, with slow, reluctant, amourous delay, for until this summer I held A. Johnson among the greatest and best of men. The carmagnoles of this recent stumping tour of his, the indecent demagogical blather he let off at every railroad station throughout the West, satisfied me that he was no statesman and that the people could not trust him as a leader. But I still believed him honest. He has so used his appointing power of late that I begin to believe him in dishonest league with rebels, and with rebel sympathizers. Loyal men (like George P. Putnam) who stood by the national cause in its darkest days are displaced, and the vilest Copperheads succeed them. This is exasperating. Mr. Ruggles thinks these state elections will prove a great cataclysm drowning A. Johnson and his "policy." God grant it!

November 5

I am more annoyed than need be, perhaps, by this stolid inaction of the College Board, and feel myself tempted to have nothing more to do with College concerns. Our corporate disease is deep-seated and incurable. The board undertakes to do a great deal that should be left to the faculty, but two-thirds of the trustees care nothing for the College and are disinclined to do any work for it. They have not the least inclination to push its interests actively and keep its affairs in public view. To attend our monthly meetings, when attendance is perfectly convenient, is to them the whole duty of a trustee. At these meetings they are always disposed to vote down or postpone any movement toward extension or invigoration, on any objection, however frivolous and unsubstantial. For they are not in earnest about the expansion and development of the College and its schools. I'm a conservative, but I believe the College would gain ground if its charter were annulled and its trustees elected annually by its alumni.

Columbia College, engraving, 1885. Hamilton Hall, the collegiate Gothic building at Madison Avenue and 50th Street was added to the old Columbia campus after Strong's time as trustee of the college, but a decade later the college would move to its present site on Morningside Heights. (*Harper's*)

DECEMBER 28

Mr. Ruggles has just happened in at eleven-thirty this evening. Spent an hour and smoked a cigar in the library. Talked of the Paris Exposition, and so on. Were I not a vestryman but a mere average Christian, I should say d— the "Exposition." It is a skillful operation of Louis Napoleon's (that imperial Barnum) designed to bring people from all the nations of the earth to his imperial capital to spend money in the shops and the lodging houses of that infamous city. The device will succeed. Paris is all "engaged" already. Its citizens are preparing to abandon their homes for a time that they may let them to Englishers and Yankees, Russians, Turks, Jews, and dwellers in Mesopotamia. On the whole, I am rather glad I have not money enough to go to Paris this spring. I should like well enough to visit Paris or any other ancient capital, but I do not want to see Paris in days of joy and jubilation and profit. I know a little of the record of Paris in the day of Marat and Couthon and Barère, and nowhere in Europe for a thousand years of war and revolution and insurrection did the great central fire of hate and murder and all abominations ever break through the crust of social charity and humane instincts so violently and so cruelly as in Paris seventy years ago. That city has been a maleficent blow-hole of poisonous gas over all Europe and over all the world since the days of Henry IV. Louis IX seems to have been the last Christian ruler of France. *He* was a soldier and a gentleman (*vide* Joinville). This Louis Napoleon seems to be neither.

1867

JANUARY 30

When I got home, I found . . . Colonel [Adam] Badeau, of General Grant's staff, just from Washington. He is sensible and observant, and his talk has additional value as probably reflecting unconsciously the views of his chief and of headquarters. His sympathies are with Congress rather than with the President. He thinks the latter well-meaning, but mulish or pig-headed; the former (or its extreme Radical element) a little violent; impeachment probable, and probably leading to grave complications. Grant says (*teste* Badeau) that he has never felt so anxious about the country as at this time. He may well feel anxious. The majority of the House seems bent on impeaching A. Johnson. (N. B. His proper classical parallel seems to be R. Spurius Furius, whose name occurs in Roman history, somewhere during the Samnite War or the First Punic War, I think. But my Roman history is very rusty.) This impeachment will be regular and constitutional. But the House may be so deluded as to take the untenable ground that a President impeached is *ipso facto* suspended from all official functions before conviction and even before trial. Should it take this ground, A. Johnson will recalcitrate. The general-in-chief will have to choose whom he and his staff and subordinates will serve, Congress or President. A. Johnson will invoke the army and navy of the United States to sustain him in his place, and Grant must take one side or the other in our "Second Civil War." On this question, A. Johnson would be right. Badeau says that the South is as cantankerous as it was in 1860 and grows more vitriolic every day. Only remedy, martial law from the Potomac to the Rio Grande; a heroic remedy that may destroy republican institutions. But Badeau thinks the people bent on preserving national unity at any cost whatever; "republican institutions," the axiomatic democratic truths of seventy years ago, are losing credit in A.D. eighteen-sixty-seven. *Teste* the Albany "Commissions" that tend to save this city from utter destruction by the votes of an ignorant, corrupt mob of brute Irish voters, bought up, systematically, by the blackguards and swindlers who infest the City Hall. We do not hold certain political "truths" quite so self-evident as we did ninety years ago; as between Thomas Jefferson and Thomas Carlyle, I'm not sure but I prefer the latter!

MAY 21

Sergeant Boston Corbett, carte-de-visite of the man who killed John Wilkes Booth. Strong speculated that in Booth's agonized flight he hoped only to "escape the gallows and to die in conflict with his pursuers." (GEH)

The pencil memoranda found in J. Wilkes Booth's pocket diary, written down during his dismal flight from the scene of his great crime and now first published, are most interesting. It seems clear that when the poor wretch commenced his flight, he was fully and serenely satisfied that his fearful crime was an act of Roman heroism, patriotism, and virtue, but that a dismal change of feeling was soon brought on him by the abhorrence with which he was regarded even by the unrepentant rebels of Virginia, whose sympathy and shelter were his sole reliance. Even poor Dr. Mudd's professional aid seems to have been given with ill-concealed aversion and unwillingness. All this seems to have opened the eyes of the murderer. Instead of comparing himself with Brutus and Tell, as he does in his first memorandum (and to his own advantage), he prays, in the second, that God may "try and forgive" him, for, as he infers from the demeanor of the men he has discoursed during his flight, his crime must be, or at least may be, outside the range of God's mercy. The assassin fairly avows at last that he felt the curse of Cain upon him, and saw no prospect but that of speedy death as a criminal. He thought of riding back into Washington and surrendering himself to the Provost-Marshal. What a ride Booth must have had through the dismal woods of Virginia, after the murder! He was tortured by a broken limb, "tearing the flesh at every jump" of his horse, tortured still worse by discovering that nobody thought his grand, heroic Roman pistol shot anything better than a pitiful, cowardly assassination, and looking forward to speedy capture and certain death. This fugitive horseman, with a wicked, unprovoked murder ten days old behind him, a broken limb tormenting his body, and misgivings about the past tormenting his soul, riding on under all manner of torture—bodily and mental—hoping only to escape the gallows and to die in conflict with his pursuers (as he did), this wretched outcast is a subject for some "sensational" painter. Gustave Doré could do justice to it. I can conceive how Gustave Doré would treat the subject: the jaded horse, the wearied rider, the ghastly pine trees, and through their branches, perhaps, a glimpse of setting sunlight resting on a distant clearing, over which blue-coated cavalrymen ride in pursuit.

Ellie and the boys went to Brattleboro this morning. I lay in bed, nauseated and wretched, as I have been these last three days.

I am *living beyond my income,* pauperizing Johnny and his little brothers. That is what's slowly killing me, and killing me by slow torture. Ellie is quite ready to give up every social enjoyment of her own. She would give them up most cheerfully. Of course, her little parties and socialities are my ruin, but I would rather die than ask her to give them up and subside into a dull, humdrum existence. These things are her life, after the interests of her children and her husband. If I cannot afford her these social enjoyments, the sooner I die the better, and I fear I can afford them no longer. So I am the less unhappy about these daily recurring pains and aches. My incapacity for work and duty grows worse every day. I confess myself "played out," and "used up." My only hope is in the fact that our Lord raised men from the dead. I am in living death. Without His Almighty saving help, I have no hope at all.

Tonight's *Post* announces the professor's (Anthon's) death. I did not expect him to last so long. . . .

How well I remember his style of work in the horrible old grammar school! *Scene:* twenty boys in a lecture room, no teacher yet in his place. Time, nine o'clock in the morning. Some little subdued talking and skylarking in progress. A wretched creature called "a monitor" in nominal charge, vainly beseeching his classmates to be quiet. The professor comes swiftly upstairs, full of business, with a big watch in his hand and twirling the big seal and the ribbon round his forefiner, and *loquitur:* "Too much noise here! Any names, monitor?" Monitor replies (distracted between his dread of discipline and his dread of lynching by his classmates), "No, sir. I didn't think—" Professor rejoins, Napoleonically, "I don't want to know what you think, sir. Take *this* down to Mr. Shea." *"This"* was a scrap of paper inscribed with the words "six blows" or "twelve blows," as the case might be. They were delivered by the rattan on the hand. Shea was lictor of the infernal old school and rattan-bearer. I do not think poor old James Shea liked his office much. So it was when we were in the "first Latin class" of the school. An imperfect recitation was punished by the order "Take *this* down to Mr. Shea." So was a bad weekly report. Shea was muscular, six-foot high, and I think kindhearted, though he did use to say, with the utmost aggravation of manner, as he flourished his rattan, "Now hold your hand straight, my sonny, or I may hurt your knuckles."

NOVEMBER 5

Many honest, patriotic people who exult over the downfall of slavery are startled at the prospect of Negro sovereignty south of the Potomac and Ohio, and are by no means sure they would like to see the Honorable Mr. Quashee Hampton or Sambo Davis claiming a seat in Congress as a representative or a senator from South Carolina or Mississippi. It is useless to say that this is all a prejudice against a black skin, and that if Quashee is not a gentleman and a statesman, it is because he is degraded by servitude that has lasted for generations. People hesitate about the Negro senator, not because of his dark cuticle, but because he belongs to a race the average intellect whereof is (in 1867 at least) of lower grade than ours; because we are familiar with the notion of a nigger servant, bootblack, barber, or field hand, and not familiar with that of a Negro legislator. We have had, to be sure, something of Soulouque and his court, the Duc de Marmalade, and so on, but generally with a disposition to grin, and we know little or nothing of the black barristers and assemblymen who hold their own in the British West Indies. To the Northern man of plain, ordinary, common understanding, a colored person helping to regulate our national finances and our foreign relations seems out of place and anomalous. Perhaps his unfitness for legislation (real or apparent) is caused by the tyrannous wrong to which he and his progenitors have been subjected. It is no doubt due, in very great measure, to that cause, and he is not to be blamed or despised for it. But his unfitness is believed in by most people as a fact, and they do not see that it is any the less a fact because it has been inflicted on him by the atrocious system of slavery.

1868–1869

Fanny Kemble, the great English actress and niece of the equally acclaimed Sarah Siddons, had married and left the Georgia planter, Pierce Butler.

The great event of the summer of 1868 was Strong's one and only trip to Europe in July with his brother-in-law, Hasket Derby. Ellie Strong and their three sons stayed home; presumably the latter were too young to be taken on an expensive trip planned mainly for the relaxation and health of their seriously overworked father. Unfortunately, the diarist was too busy sightseeing to do more than jot down the places of his itinerary.

The statue in Central Park referred to in Strong's entry of September 22, 1869, is of Baron Alexander von Humboldt, German naturalist and explorer of South America.

The statue of Commodore Cornelius Vanderbilt that now stands before the south façade of Grand Central Station originally occupied a niche in the colossal pediment of the Hudson River Railway Depot designed by Ernest Plassman.

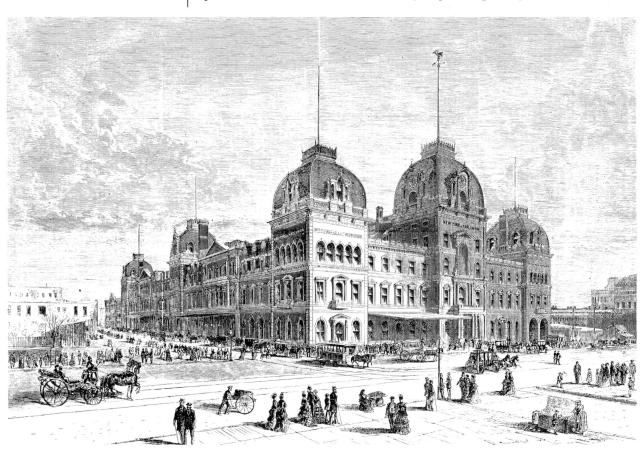

1868

APRIL 29

Last night with Ellie to the theatre appurtenant to the Union League Club-house, whilom "Jerome's Theatre," and heard Mrs. Fanny Kemble read *Cymbeline*. It was an admirable reading, but perhaps a little stagey and overdone, here and there. I am specially fond of that play, for Imogen has always seemed to me the most lovable and the very noblest of all Shakespeare's portraits of noble and lovely women. And while Mrs. Kemble read, I was obliged to fix my thoughts, sometimes, as firmly as I could, on the fooleries and buffooneries of *La Belle Hélène*, to keep myself from snivelling. Her great talent and her careful study of the text make her reading an instructive commentary upon it. She brought out many points that were new to me; for example, Imogen's question in the last scene, "Why did you throw your wedded lady from you?"—so delightfully appropriate to her loving, generous, and loyal wifely nature. I have always understood this is a cry of passionate joy uttered as she throws herself into her husband's arms. But there is far more delicacy and truth in Mrs. Kemble's rendering. She gives it in a faint, broken whisper—as the instinctive utterance of one hardly yet half conscious and only just beginning to recover from the blow that has stricken her down—without the least trace of complaint or resentment and without any intensity of expression.

Pity Mrs. Kemble is such a Tartar. The ladies (Mrs. Cooper, Mrs. Barlow, and others) at whose request she read last night, for the benefit of some charity which they administer, addressed her a very civil note, proposing to send a carriage for her, and to meet her at the door, and introduce her into the house. Mr. Tighe tells me he saw her answer. "She would be happy to read for the benefit of the (whatever it was); she needed no introduction, and she could pay her own hack-hire. Yours resp'y."

In the same key was her reply to one of the Fields, at Stockbridge, who remarked by way of civility, "Madam, you ride that horse better than I can." The reply was, "Of course. You are afraid of the horse, and the horse is afraid of *me*."

Poor Pierce Butler! I fear his married life was stormy.

OPPOSITE: **Cornelius Vanderbilt planned this earlier Grand Central Station, which was finished in 1871, to house facilities for three important railroads he had acquired since 1862. (*Harper's*)**

Rain and fog, followed by a stiff stormy northeast breeze. General stampede to deck from breakfast table to see *an iceberg*. According to Captain Hockley, it was two miles off (north), 1,400 feet high, and all the officers said it was the finest they ever saw. A great peak (like the Matterhorn, according to travelled passengers) shot up from an amorphous mass, probably more than a mile long. This peak was the color of certain pale green crystals of fluor spar. The rest of the berg was seamed with ravines and gorges, full of beautiful lights and shadows, and of exquisite tints of grey and blue. The whole thing like a huge opal. Great boulders lay on its ledges, shewing that it had drifted down from its parent glacier on some Greenland fiord without turning over. Everybody said we ought to have seen it blazing and glittering in full sunshine, but I thought it more impressive drifting down through cold fog, like a picket guard or reconnoitering party from the stern Northern sea.

1869

To Central Park this afternoon to inspect the live critters assembled in and around the old Arsenal building—the nucleus of our future Zoological Garden. The collection is not large, and consists of donations sent in and received without any system: sundry bears, black bears and a grizzly bear, prairie dogs, foxes, beautiful ocelots, owls, eagles, two meek camels, pheasants, monkeys, macaws, etc. It amounts to little. But the critters look healthy and receive much attention from visitors. Long walk tonight.

Yesterday they broke ground for the new Post Office at the south end of the City Hall Park, and today a great wooden enclosure is going up around its site. This will destroy the best-known and most characteristic street view in New York, viz., looking up from Fulton Street and Broadway across the Park to the South front of the old City Hall. "The Park" will be destroyed, but it has long survived its usefulness, except as a place for blackguard boys to pitch coppers in all day, and for thieves and ruffians to meander through all night. No reference to the Common Council.

New Post Office, City Hall Park, lithograph by Currier & Ives, n.d. Strong lamented that this building would "destroy the best-known and most characteristic street view in New York, viz., looking up from Fulton Street and Broadway across the Park to the South front of the old City Hall." (MCNY)

OVERLEAF: *The Grand Drive, Central Park, N.Y.,* lithograph by Currier & Ives, 1869. The park a dozen years after work had begun, with the old Arsenal in the background. (MCNY)

The Central Park Zoo in the
1870s, behind the Arsenal, at
Fifth Avenue and 63rd Street.
Strong inspected "the live critters
assembled in and around the old
Arsenal building" on August 10,
1868. (MCNY)

SEPTEMBER 2

Long walk tonight. I am systematically exploring the West Side Avenues, which have grown up quite out of my knowledge. The Eighth, for instance, is now a brilliant shopping street—far more brilliant than the Sixth. The Seventh seems all compact of the lowest tenement houses and whiskey mills, an elongated Five Points. This evening I lost my way completely in that enchanted region of irregular byways—Hammond Street, Jane Street, Greenwich Avenue, and so on—as I do whenever I visit it. Got myself utterly dis-oriented, and found myself at Greenwich Street, making straight for the North River, when I thought myself marching eastward and near Sixth Avenue.

SEPTEMBER 22

Apropos of the Park, I hear that many of our Teutonic fellow citizens who crowded to witness the "unveiling" or "dedication" of the bust of Humboldt near the Fifth Avenue gate supposed they were doing honor to Helmbold, the sporting druggist, who has a flashy shop on Broadway and who is said to have acquired a vast fortune by pictorial advertisements of "Humbold's Bucher" all over the city, if not the universe. The bust, by the by, is quite good, unobtrusive, and inoffensive.

OCTOBER 9

Application from three infatuated young women for admission to Law School. No woman shall degrade herself by practising law, in New York especially, if I can save her. Our committee will probably have to pass on the application, *pro forma*, but I think the clack of these possible Portias will never be heard at Dwight's moot courts. "Women's-Rights Women" are uncommonly loud and offensive of late. I loathe the lot. The first effect of their success would be the introduction into society of a third sex, without the grace of woman or the vigor of man; and then woman, being physically the weaker vessel and having thrown away the protection of her present honors and immunities, would become what the squaw is to the male of her species—a drudge and domestic animal. . . .

OPPOSITE: *The Age of Brass, or the Triumph of Woman's Rights,* lithograph by Currier & Ives, 1869. As Strong wrote in his diary, " 'Women's-Rights Women' are uncommonly loud and offensive of late. I loathe the lot." (MCNY)

NOVEMBER 11

The grand *Vanderbilt* Bronze on the Hudson River Railroad Depot "unveiled" yesterday with much solemnity. There was a prayer and there were speeches. Vanderbilt began life penniless. He acquired a competence—honestly, I assume—by energy, economy, and business tact, and then increased his store to a colossal fortune of sixty millions (as they say) by questionable operations in railroad stocks. Anyhow he is a millionaire of millionaires. And, therefore, we bow down before him, and worship him, with a hideous group of molten images, with himself for a central figure, at a cost of $800,000. These by thy Gods, O Israel! *Vide* Carlyle's Latter Day Tract entitled "Hudson's Statue." But it is not clear, after all, that this act of Idolatry and Mammon Worship—the honor thus paid to a successful money-maker as a Hero—is to be charged against the community of New York, though that community is rotten and snobbish enough for almost any conceivable baseness. The money may have been raised among Vanderbilt's jackals and subordinates. Perhaps he was himself the largest subscriber. Moreover, it is to be remembered that Vanderbilt did a grand thing or two during the war. . . .

Cornelius Vanderbilt, photograph. Strong is present at the unveiling of a statue of Vanderbilt and questions "this act of Idolatry and Mammon Worship—the honor thus paid to a successful money-maker as a Hero." (MCNY)

DECEMBER 18

...N. B. Barnard and Cardozo (*arcades ambo*) seem to have fallen out a little. The stink of our state judiciary is growing too strongly ammoniac and hippuric for endurance. Like Trinculo, we "do smell all h—p—" whenever we read or hear of the sayings or doings of the average New York judge. He is as bad as the New York alderman, if not worse, because his office is more sacred. People begin to tire of holding their noses, and are looking about in a helpless way for some remedy. The nuisance must be abated somehow and that soon, but I see no hope of its abatement, except by a most perilous process, justified only by the extremest necessity, and after all constitutional remedies are exhausted. Some change is certainly needed most urgently. Law protects life no longer. Any scoundrel who is backed by a little political influence in the corner groceries of his ward can commit murder with almost absolute impunity. The sheriff's office is a den of Celtic thieves, roughs, and *Sicarii.* Law does not protect property. The abused machinery of Law is a terror to property owners. No banker or merchant is sure that some person, calling himself a "receiver," appointed *ex parte* as the first step in some frivolous suit he never heard of, may not march into his counting room at any moment, demand possession of all his assets and the ruinous suspension of his whole business, and when the order for a receiver is vacated a week afterwards, claim $100,000 or so as "an allowance" for his services, by virtue of another order, to be enforced by attachment. No city can long continue rich and prosperous that tolerates abuses like these. Capital will flee to safer quarters.

1870–1875

This was the era of the coming of age of New York as a great cultural capital and the founding of its vital centers of science, arts, and letters: The American Museum of Natural History in 1869, the Metropolitan Museum of Art in 1870, and the Lenox Library (now the New York Public Library) in 1877.

John Jacob Astor, a son of William B. Astor and father of the Waldorf Astor who moved to England and became Viscount Astor, was a close friend of Strong's.

"Jim" Fisk was the dishonest stock manipulator who with Jay Gould gained control of the Erie Railroad from Cornelius Vanderbilt and almost succeeded in cornering the gold market in 1869, which had disastrous effects on the nation's business.

Strong's last years were troubled with nagging ill health, and an enlarged liver proved fatal on July 21, 1875, when he was aged only fifty-five.

JANUARY 25, TUESDAY

At half-past ten last evening, Delano, wending his way home from a dinner at John Astor's, was set upon and robbed by three men on the corner of Fifth Avenue and Eleventh Street. Of course there was no arrest. Crime was never so bold, so frequent, and so safe as it is this winter. We breathe an atmosphere of highway robbery, burglary, and murder. Few criminals are caught, and fewer punished. Municipal law is a failure in New York, and we must soon fall back on the law of self-preservation. Among the most prominent candidates for informal execution are sundry ministers of justice—or rather of injustice—the most notorious scoundrels out of jail and far more nefarious than most who are in it. Secret, irresponsible tribunals are ugly and dangerous, as witness the English trades-unions, but they may become necessity. . . .

MARCH 17

One Revels, an Ethiop from Mississippi (or perhaps only a mulatto or octoroon), has been making a speech in his place as U.S. Senator. Ten years ago we should have thought a Feejee president not more absurdly improbable. The world does move, and the arrogant folly of Southern swashbucklers and fanatics in 1860 and 1861 gave it a shove such as it had not felt for centuries. The French Revolution took more time, and its causes had been longer at work. O Jeff Davis, ain't this a go? What do you think of the "genman" who sits in your seat and represents your own—your be-yutious, your chivalr-r-r-ric—state? To this have all your intriguings and blusterings and proclamations and conscriptions come at last! . . .

OCTOBER 13

Died at Lexington, Virginia, the ex-Rebel General, Robert E. Lee, whom it is the fashion to laud and magnify as one of the greatest and best of men. But a chief of staff who resigns his commission and instantly transfers himself to an enemy's service, taking with him all the military secrets of his commander and all the information he had acquired in his place of high trust, is not a man whom I delight to honor. A counsel who should throw up his brief for the plaintiff the day before the case was set down for trial and take a retainer on the other side would be hooted by his brethren and silenced by the court. I refer to a decent bench and a respectable bar, not to our New York institutions. But such a proceeding would hardly be tolerated, even here. How does it differ in principle from Lee's course in April, 1861?

General Robert E. Lee, lithograph from *The Heroes of the Civil War*, 1888.

1871

JANUARY 10

Jim Fisk's last recorded antic was on New Year's Day. He made calls in a gorgeous chariot drawn by four high-stepping horses, with four smart footmen in flamboyant liveries. When he stopped before any favored house, his mamelukes descended, unrolled a carpet, laid it from the carriage steps to the door, and stood on either side in attitude of military salute, while their august master passed by. It is a queer world, and this is a "devilish lively" community.

APRIL 29

Nasty affair at the Four-in-Hand Club the other night over a midnight card table, at which Henry Brevoort lost some eight hundred dollars. He was stimulated by this misfortune grossly and gratuitously to insult William Jay (John Jay's son), a good-natured fellow who was innocently looking on. Jay knocked him down, the others interfered, and Brevoort carried away an ensanguined countenance and has not been heard from since. Some say that a challenge from him would be declined because his pistol discharged itself out of due time when he fought a duel with one Calhoun at Paris, which may be true or may not. All this story is printed in great detail by the scandal-mongering *Sun* newspaper. I remember Brevoort telling me last fall that he had some weighty grievance against some of the members or committees of this club; hence, probably, his bloody nose.

JUNE 3

... Visited this afternoon the Metropolitan Museum of Art in the late Mrs. Douglas Cruger's palazzo on West Fourteenth Street. The Cesnola collection of antiquities from Cyprus is interesting and large. Some of the glass vessels are exquisitely colored with iridescence from partial decomposition or disintegration of the surface, I suppose. The gallery of "Old Masters" is not exciting to behold, Johnston has deposited Turner's "Slave Ship" there. A large quantity

The Sculpture Gallery of the Metropolitan Museum of Art on West 14th Street. Strong predicts that this "collection promises very well, indeed. Twenty years hence it will probably have grown into a really instructive museum." (MCNY)

of "articles of bigotry and virtue"—namely, vases, arms, odd china, and the like—has also been loaned by Sam Barlow, Meredith Howland, Kennedy, and others. Some of these things are costly and curious. The specimens of early printing are good (there is a Caxton among them!), and there are a few little volumes of MS *Hours.* Art treasures (so-called) are evidently accumulating in New York, being picked up in Europe by our millionaires and brought home. This collection promises very well, indeed. Twenty years hence it will probably have grown into a really instructive museum.

JULY 22

These three cases of George A. Jones, Taintor, and Mills, all occurring within so short a time, show how thoroughly even our so-called best people are demoralized by the prevalent passion for acquiring the maximum of money in the minimum of time. *"Qui volunt divites fieri, incidunt in loqueum diaboli,"* saith the Vulgate. Great-wealth, unless inherited, or acquired by professional energy and industry, is now, as a general rule, presumptive evidence against the character of its owner. . . . Most of the dodges, devices, and complots which Wall Street considers legitimate and in which millions are lost and won (on paper) every day, are, of course, plainly guileful, dishonest, and wicked. But how many of our nice, fresh, ingenuous boys are plunged into this filthy pool every year at eighteen or even younger . . . though their parents can well afford them a liberal education. Each hopes to win some great prize in that great gambling house, an establishment far less honest than were those of Baden-Baden and Homburg. And so they grow up to be mere illiterate sharpers, with possible fine houses and fine horses and fine Newport cottages and without capacity to appreciate anything higher—men without culture and with damaged and dwarfed moral sense.

1874

JUNE 13

With dear Lucy and Louis last night to Booth's Theatre to see Salvini's *Othello.* He is excellently well supported, and his is a wonderful piece of acting. Nobody ever made such play with his eyes or converted himself into so close a semblance of Satan. It's a muscular performance. Of course, he overacts a good deal, condescending to the taste of an uncultured audience. I fear I quite cut myself out of dear little Lucy's good graces by humbly submitting that I rather thought so, in reply to her query. . . . In the finale, Othello turns from the audience and saws away like fury at his own throat with a great snickersnee he happens to have about him, an improvement on the obviously innocuous dagger of the ordinary stage suicide, and drops very handsomely. As the curtain descends, he is heard to gurgle or wheeze, as his breath escapes through the lacerated larynx, and he is seen to be kicking tremulously with his left leg. All which is powerful and *magnifique,* but not art. It was a very fine and telling impersonation, nevertheless. The house was jammed and enthusiastic. . . .

Booth's Theater, engraving. The best-equipped theater in New York, it was opened by Edwin Booth in 1868 on the southeast corner of Sixth Avenue and 23rd Street. The great actor went bankrupt in the Panic of 1873, and by 1883 the theater had been converted into a department store. (MCNY)

Busy day at 187 Fulton Street. Dined here Bagnotti (Italian vice-consul, I believe); also, the great Salvini, Mr. Ruggles, and Dick. . . . Salvini is genial and gentlemanlike. I gave him my thanks as a commentator on Shakespeare, which he received simply and nicely. There is no pretension about him, nor any affectation of grandeur.

1875

JUNE 12, SATURDAY

I finally broke down two days after my last entry, Saturday, the 15th, being unable to eat, hardly able to stand, and suffering constant sharp pain. I authorized Ellie to send for Dr. Peters, which I should have done a month before. Peters appeared and forthwith told me frankly that I was in very considerable danger, and that if I had delayed sending for him another week, he could probably have done nothing in the premises. The trouble was not dyspepsia but a liver enlarged to about three times its normal bulk, like that of a Strassburg gander, and threatening "induration," cirrhosis, and dropsy. I don't think the danger of all this quite over yet, but Peters thinks it diminishing and that, though I'm still on a lee shore, I am slowly clawing off in a hopeful way. He continues vigilant and most vigorous in his requirements as to diet and medicine.

JUNE 23

Much warmer. I have been losing ground this last week, am as weak as I was a month ago, and have lost taste for all food save milk, of which emollient fluid I ingurgitate two full quarts per diem. Peters is to bring Dr. Alonzo Clark to inspect me tomorrow.

JUNE 25, FRIDAY

A hot day. Peters brought the great Dr. Alonzo Clark yesterday, who manipulated my liver with great energy but pronounced no definite judgment that I heard of. I have been improving the wrong way, like bad fish in warm weather. One day last week, I had a woeful day of headache, nausea, and malaise, which left me as weak as a sea anemone at low water. Since then, there has been no improvement.

This was the diarist's last entry; he died on July 21.

A
Bibliographic
History

The Diary of Philip Hone, 1828–1851. 2 vols. Edited by Bayard Tuckerman. 1889. Reprint (2 vols. in 1). New York: Dodd, Mead and Co., 1910.

The Diary of Philip Hone, 1828–1851. 2 vols. Edited by Allan Nevins. New York: Dodd, Mead and Co., 1927. Reprint (2 vols. in 1). Salem, N.H.: Arno Press, 1970.

The Diary of Philip Hone, 1828–1851. Rev. ed. 2 vols. Edited by Allan Nevins. New York: Dodd, Mead & Co., 1936.

The Diary of George Templeton Strong. 4 vols. Edited by Allan Nevins and Milton Halsey Thomas. New York: Macmillan Publishing Co., 1952. Reprint. New York: Hippocrene Books, 1970.

The Diary of George Templeton Strong. Abridged ed. Edited by Allan Nevins and Milton Halsey Thomas. Seattle, Wash.: University of Washington Press, 1987.

Acknowledgments

For invaluable aid in illustrating and producing this volume, the following people deserve full credit:

At Abbeville Press, Walton Rawls, Lisa Peyton, Massoumeh Farmaian, Mark Magowan, Robin James, Hope Koturo, and the designer Joel Avirom.

At the Museum of the City of New York, Bonnie Yochelson, Terry Ariano, and Cathy McGee.

At the New-York Historical Society, Cammie Naylor.

Thanks are also due the staffs of the New York Public Library, the Library of Congress, the Smithsonian Institution, and the Metropolitan Museum of Art.

Index

Italic page references indicate artwork or photographs.